True Stories

4

Sandra Heyer

True Stories: Level 4, Silver Edition

Pearson Education, 221 River Street, Hoboken, NJ 07030

Staff Credits: The people who made up the *True Stories: Level 4, Silver Edition* team, representing content creation, design, manufacturing, marketing, multimedia, project management, publishing, rights management, and testing, are Pietro Alongi, Tracey Cataldo, Dave Dickey, Warren Fischbach, Lucy Hart, Gosia Jaros-White, Barry Katzen, Linda Moser, Dana Pinter, Paula Van Ells, Joseph Vella, and Peter West.

Text design and layout: Don Williams
Composition: Page Designs International
Project supervision: Bernard Seal
Contributing editors: Françoise Leffler and Bernard Seal

Cover images *(top to bottom)* Photobank gallery/Shutterstock; DisobeyArt/Shutterstock; Luc Kohnen/Shutterstock; Tiffany Bryant/Shutterstock; atosan/123RF; (silver edition badge) deepstock/Shutterstock.

Interior images Page 2: Amophoto_au/Shutterstock; 12: Ed Wray/AP Images; 21: *(tl)* Dmitry Travnikov/123RF, *(tr)* Photobank gallery/Shutterstock, *(b)* Alexander Mazurkevich/Shutterstock; 22: DisobeyArt/Shutterstock; 30: *(acupuncture needles)* Bjoern Wylezich/Shutterstock, *(goldfish)* Dien/Shutterstock; 36: *(people top to bottom)* Kurhan/123RF, Gstockstudio/123RF, Allison Hays/123RF, *(positive and negative emojis)* I.sedano/Shutterstock; 37: *(people top to bottom)* Dubova/Shutterstock, Cathy Yeulet/123RF, mastakas/123RF, Maridav/Shutterstock, WAYHOME studio/Shutterstock, Sylv1rob1/Shutterstock, *(positive and negative emojis)* I.sedano/Shutterstock; 38: Courtesy of Natalie Garibian; 43: Ivsanmas/Shutterstock; 48: Stelian Porojnicu/123RF; 55: *(tl)* Luc Kohnen/Shutterstock, *(tr)* G. Dagli Orti/De Agostini Picture Library/Getty Images, *(ml)* AKGImages, *(mr)* Perspectivestock/Shutterstock, *(b)* Chris and Sally Gable/LatitudeStock/Alamy Stock Photo; 56: Rido/Shutterstock; 64: Annie Pratt; 70: *(t)* Science & Society Picture Library/Getty Images, *(b)* Jeff J Mitchell/Getty Images News/Getty Images; 71: *(t)* White House Photo/Alamy Stock Photo, *(b)* Zoonar/edpics/Zoonar GmbH/Alamy Stock Photo; 72: Tiffany Bryant/Shutterstock; 74: *(tl)* ConceptVectorDesign/Shutterstock, *(tr)* Demja/Shutterstock; 80: Atosan/123RF; 86: *(icons top to bottom)* Kittisak Taramas/123RF, Khoon Lay Gan/123RF, Anastasia Ivlicheva/123RF, Yuliya Belenkova/123RF, Tul Chalothonrangsee/123RF; 88: Daxus/E+/Getty Images; 96: Monkey Business Images/Shutterstock; 104: Gabor Kovacs Photography/Shutterstock; 111: *(tl)* Michael Francis McElroy/ZUMA Press, Inc./Alamy Stock Photo, *(ml)* Moviestore/REX/Shutterstock, *(bl)* America/Alamy Stock Photo, *(tr)* George Sheldon/Shutterstock, *(br)* HKPNC/Getty Images; 112: Ronnie Kaufman/Blend Images/Getty Images; 120: Gau Meo/Shutterstock; 128: Katarzyna Bialasiewicz/123RF; 130: Nigel Marple/AP Images; 136: *(t)* Rich Clarkson & Associates/NCAA Photos/Getty Images, *(b)* Getty Images Sport/Getty Images; 137: S&G/PA Images/Alamy Stock Photo.

Illustrations Don Martinetti

Map Page 16: Aptara

Library of Congress Cataloging-in-Publication Data

A catalog record for the print edition is available from the Library of Congress.

Printed in the United States of America

ISBN-10: 0-13-5177944
ISBN-13: 978-0-13-5177945

1   18

CONTENTS

INTRODUCTION

TRUE STORIES, SILVER EDITION

The Silver Edition of *True Stories* is a five-level reading series. The series is appropriate for low-beginning to high-intermediate learners of English as a Second or Foreign Language. The Silver Edition consists of revised editions of six of the highly successful and popular *True Stories in the News* books that have provided entertaining stories and effective reading skill instruction for many years. In fact, the first book in that series was published over twenty-five years ago (hence the title "Silver" Edition). The *True Stories* series has been going strong ever since.

NEW IN THE SILVER EDITION

- **New and updated stories.** Some stories have been updated, and some have been replaced with fresh new readings that have been thoroughly classroom-tested before making it into print. All of the readings that have proven to be favorites of students and teachers over the years have been retained.

- **A colorful new design.** Originally published solely in black and white, the new edition has a new full-color design with colorful new photos. The color design makes the readings even more inviting, and the color photos that accompany the readings enhance understanding and enjoyment of the stories.

- **A uniform unit structure.** The books in the series have been given a consistent unit structure that runs across all six books. This predictable structure makes it easy for teachers to teach the series at different levels and for students to progress seamlessly from one level to the next.

- **Audio recordings of every reading.** Every story in the series has been recorded and made available online for students or teachers to download.

- **Online Answer Keys and To the Teacher notes.** The Answer Keys are now online as downloadable pdfs. Teachers may provide these to the students should they wish. In addition, the To the Teacher notes that were previously in the back of the books are now online. This section provides additional information about the stories and teaching tips. Additional practice activities are also now available online.

THE APPROACH

The underlying premise in this series has always been that when second language learners are engaged in a pleasurable reading experience in the second language, then language learning will take place effortlessly and effectively. The formula is simple: Offer students a true story that fascinates and surprises them. Have them read and enjoy the story. Focus their attention on some useful vocabulary in the story. Confirm that they fully understand the story with reading comprehension exercises. Develop reading skills that progress from basic to more complex. Finally, use the content and the topic of the story to engage in discussion and writing tasks, from tightly structured to more open-ended.

UNIT COMPONENTS

Pre-Reading

Each unit begins with a pre-reading task that piques students' curiosity about the content of the story. Students' attention is drawn to the art that accompanies the reading and the title of the reading as they predict what the story is going to be about.

Reading

The readings are short enough to be read by the students in class; at the lower levels, the stories can be read in minutes. As the levels become higher, the readings do become longer and more challenging. Still, even at the highest levels, each reading and the exercises immediately following it can be completed in one class meeting.

Post-Reading

While there is some variation in the post-reading activities, the following are in all six books:

- **Vocabulary.** Useful key vocabulary items are selected from the readings for presentation and practice. The vocabulary activities vary from unit to unit, and the number of vocabulary items and the extent of the practice increases from level to level.

- **Comprehension.** At least two different comprehension tasks follow the vocabulary section. The exercises have descriptive titles, such as Understanding the Main Ideas, Remembering Details, or Understanding Cause and Effect, so that teachers and students know which cognitive skills are being applied. The exercises have a great deal of variety, keeping students engaged and motivated.

- **Discussion.** Having read and studied the stories, students are encouraged to discuss some aspect arising from the story. Even at the lowest level, students are given simple tasks that will give them the opportunity to talk in pairs, in small groups, or as a whole class.

- **Writing.** The final section of each unit has students produce a short piece of writing related to the reading. Often the writing task derives directly from the Discussion, in which case the title of the section is Discussion/Writing. The writing tasks are level-appropriate and vary in complexity depending on student proficiency. The tasks are not intended to be graded. They simply provide a final opportunity for students to engage with the topic of the reading and deepen their understanding and enjoyment of the story.

TRUE STORIES, LEVEL 4

True Stories, Level 4 is the fifth book in the *True Stories*, Silver Edition series. It is intended for intermediate learners of English. It consists of 16 eight- to ten-page units, each with the following distinguishing features:

- The pre-reading task has students look at a photo that prompts them to speculate on the content of the story.

- Each story has an average length of 3,000 words.

- Writing exercises require students to write a dialog, a letter, a description, or a short essay about a personal experience.

- Two-page "Challenge" readings at the end of every unit are at a slightly higher level and prepare students for the transition from controlled to authentic written English.

ACKNOWLEDGMENTS

I would like to thank

- the many teachers whose invaluable feedback helped me assess how the stories and exercises were working outside the small sphere of my own classroom. If I were to list you all by name, this acknowledgments section would go on for pages. I would like to thank three colleagues in particular: legendary teacher Peggy Miles, who introduced me to the world of English language teaching; Sharron Bassano, whose innovative techniques for teaching beginning-level students informed my own approach; and Jorge Islas Martinez, whose enthusiasm and dedication remain a constant inspiration;

- my students, who shared personal stories that became the examples for the discussion and writing exercises;

- the people in the stories who supplied details that were not in news sources: Twyla Thompson, John Koehler, Dorothy Peckham, Chi Hsii Tsui, Margaret Patrick, Trish Moore and Rhonda Gill (grandmother and mother of Desiree), Friendship Force participants, Natalie Garibian, Mirsada Buric, and the late Irvin Scott;

- the teachers and editors who made important contributions at different stages of development to the previous editions of these books and whose influence can still be seen throughout this new edition: Allen Ascher, John Barnes, Karen Davy, Joanne Dresner, Nancy Hayward, Stacey Hunter, Penny LaPorte, Laura LeDrean, Françoise Leffler, Linda Moser, Dana Klinek Pinter, Mary Perrotta Rich, Debbie Sistino, and Paula Van Ells;

- Rachel Hayward and Megan Hohenstein, who assisted in piloting and researching new material for the Silver Edition;

- the team at Pearson, whose experienced hands skillfully put together all the moving pieces in the preparation of this Silver Edition: Pietro Alongi, Tracey Cataldo, Warren Fischbach, Lucy Hart, Gosia Jaros-White, Linda Moser, Dana Pinter, Joseph Vella, and Peter West;

- copyeditor and fact checker, Kate Smyres; and proofreader, Ann Dickson;

- editor extraordinaire Françoise Leffler, who lent her expertise to *True Stories* levels 4 and 5;

- Bernard Seal at Page Designs International, who guided this project from start to finish with dedication, creativity, pragmatism, and the occasional "crazy"—but brilliant—idea;

- Don Williams at Page Designs International, whose talent for design is evident on every page; and

- my husband, John Hajdu Heyer, who read the first draft of every story I've considered for the *True Stories* series. The expression on his face as he read told me whether or not the story was a keeper. He didn't know that. Now he does.

FROM THE AUTHOR

Dear Teachers and Students,

This new edition of *True Stories* is the Silver
Edition because it celebrates an anniversary—
it has been more than 25 years since the first
True Stories book was published. The way we
get our news has changed a lot over the years,
but some things have remained the same:
Fascinating stories are in the news every day,
and the goal of the *True Stories* series is still to bring the best of them
to you.

The question students ask most often about these stories is *Are they true?*
The answer is *yes*—to the best of my knowledge, these stories are true.
I've fact-checked stories by contacting reporters, photojournalists, and
research librarians all over the world. I've even called some of the people
in the stories to be sure I have the facts right.

Once I'm as sure as I can be that a story is true, the story has to pass
one more test. My students read the story, and after they finish reading,
they give each story one, two, or three stars. They take this responsibility
seriously; they know that only the top-rated stories will become part of
the *True Stories* reading series.

I hope that you, too, think these are three-star stories. And I hope that
reading them encourages you to share your own stories, which are always
the most amazing true stories of all.

Sandra Heyer

UNIT 1

1 PRE-READING

Think about these questions. Discuss your answers with your classmates.

1. Look at the title of the story. What does *love at first sight* mean?

2. Do you believe people can fall in love "at first sight"?

3. Do you know anyone who fell in love at first sight? Tell the class the story.

Love at First Sight

When Pamela Claypole was 56 years old, her whole life changed. She was outside working in her garden on a Saturday morning when suddenly she felt dizzy. That's all she remembers. Neighbors found her lying on the ground, unconscious. At a nearby hospital, doctors made their diagnosis: Pamela had had a stroke. She couldn't move the left side of her body, and she couldn't see, hear, or speak. Gradually, she got better. In a few months, she was able to use the left side of her body again, and she was able to hear and speak. But she still couldn't see. Her doctors told her she might be blind for the rest of her life.

Pamela came home from the hospital and began learning to live without her sight. It wasn't easy. Pamela was single, and she lived alone. There were days when she wished she hadn't survived the stroke. But as time went on, she began to adjust. She learned to take care of herself—to cook, to clean, to shop. There were just a few things she couldn't do. She couldn't fix things in her house, for example. When something broke, her friends had to help her.

One morning about three years after her stroke, Pamela was washing dishes and realized that the water wasn't going down the drain in her kitchen sink. It was probably clogged. "Call Mitch," her friends told her. Mitch was the local handyman. He fixed things for people and helped them with jobs around the house. He was middle-aged and single, and he loved his work.

Pamela called Mitch. "I hear you're a pretty good plumber," she said. "I've got a problem with my kitchen sink. Can you come over?"

"I'll be right there," Mitch told her. He fixed the sink in just a few minutes. "All done," he said.

"Thank you. How much do I owe you?" Pamela asked.

"Nothing," Mitch said. "But a cup of tea would be nice."

Pamela made some tea, and she and Mitch sat at her kitchen table and talked. He told her he would be happy to help her anytime.

Over the next two years, Mitch came to Pamela's house often to fix something or to work with her in the garden. He never accepted a penny from Pamela for the work he did; he said a cup of tea and a little conversation were payment enough. The truth was that Mitch was in love with Pamela. He never told her, though. Mitch was not a handsome man. "If she could see me," he thought, "she wouldn't love me."

One morning Pamela woke up early. She turned her head on the pillow and saw the hands on the alarm clock next to her bed: 5:30 a.m. She could see! She ran to the front door of her house and looked outside. She could see the flowers, the trees, the houses across the street. She cried with happiness. Then she went to the phone and called her best friend, Mitch.

"Hello, Mitch," she said. "It's an emergency! Come quick!"

Mitch thought about Pamela's phone call as he threw on some clothes. What kind of emergency could there be at 5:30 in the morning? Was there water everywhere? Was someone trying to break into her house? He ran the half mile to Pamela's house.

Pamela opened the front door. "Pam, are you okay?" Mitch said. Pamela looked at him and smiled. "Your eyes are brown," she said.

"What?" he asked.

"Your eyes are brown," she repeated.

"You can see?"

"Yes!" Pamela said and threw her arms around Mitch. Mitch was happy for Pamela, and he was also happy for himself. "She can see me, and she still likes me," he thought.

A few weeks later, Mitch asked Pamela to marry him, and she said yes. He told her that he had loved her from the first moment he saw her, when he came to fix her sink.

"Why didn't you ever tell me?" Pamela asked him.

"I thought you wouldn't want me because I'm not handsome," Mitch said.

"I don't care what you look like," Pamela told Mitch. "I've loved you for years."

"Well, why didn't you tell me?" he asked.

"I thought you wouldn't want me," she answered, "because I was blind."

2 VOCABULARY

LOOKING AT THE STORY

Complete the sentences with the words below.

accepted	dizzy	nearby	stroke
adjust	handyman	owe	threw on some clothes
clogged	might	sight	unconscious
come over			

1. Pamela was working in her garden when suddenly it seemed that everything was going around and around. She felt _____*dizzy*_____ .

2. When neighbors found Pamela, her eyes were closed and she was lying on the ground. They couldn't wake her up. She was *unconscious*

3. Neighbors took Pamela to a _____*nearby*_____ hospital. It was only a mile from her house.

4. Pamela couldn't move the left side of her body, and she couldn't hear, speak, or see. She had had a _____*stroke*_____ .

5. Pamela asked her doctors, "Will I see again?" They said, "We're not sure." They told her she _____*might*_____ be blind for the rest of her life.

6. When Pamela came home from the hospital, she couldn't see. It was difficult to live without her _____*sight*_____ .

7. Pamela had to change the ways she did things. She had to learn new ways of cleaning, cooking, and shopping. She had to _____*adjust*_____ to being blind.

8. Mitch fixed things for people and helped them with small jobs around the house. He was a _____*handyman*_____ .

9. Pamela wanted Mitch to come to her house to fix the sink. So she called him and asked, "Can you _____*come over*_____ ?"

10. The water wasn't going down in the sink because there was something in the drain. The drain was _____*clogged*_____ .

11. Pamela wanted to know the cost after Mitch fixed her sink. "How much do I _____*owe*_____ you?" she asked.

12. Mitch didn't take any money for his work. He never _____*accepted*_____ a penny.

13. Pamela called Mitch and said, "It's an emergency! Come quick!" Mitch didn't take time to dress carefully. He just _____*threw on some*_____ and ran to Pamela's house.

LOOKING AT A NEW CONTEXT

A Read these sentences. If the sentence is true for you, check (✓) *YES*. If it is not true for you, check (✓) *NO*. Explain your *YES* answers. Write your explanations on the lines. Here, for example, is what one student wrote about a *YES* sentence.

	YES	NO

Someone owes me money. ☑ ☐

My brother owes me $200.

1. I have been unconscious. ☐ ☒

I have been unconscious for a second.

2. I need a handyman to do some work in my home. ☐ ☒

Tam helped me to repair my fridy.

3. I know someone who had a stroke. ☒ ☐

My mom had a stroke 10 years ago.

4. Sometimes I just throw on some clothes and don't take time to dress carefully. ☐ ☒

Moust days I'm in harry and don't time To dress carefully.

5. This year I had to adjust to something new. ☒ ☐

I had adjusted my new T.V. set this year.

6. I owe someone some money. ☐ ☒

I owe one of my friends $100.

7. Someone owes me money. ☐ ☒

My best friend owes me $10,000

8. A lot of my relatives live nearby. ☐ ☒

Most of my family members are living nearby.

9. Sometimes I do not accept money for the work I do. ☐ ☐

I do works for free sometimes.

10. I know how to fix a clogged drain. ☐ ☐

My son has fixed his kitchen clogged drain.

11. Sometimes I feel dizzy. ☐ ☒

I felt dizzy yesterday.

B Share your *YES* answers in a small group.

3 COMPREHENSION / READING SKILLS

FORMING MENTAL IMAGES AS YOU READ

Do you see pictures in your mind as you read? Look at these pictures. Find the sentence in the story that goes with each picture. Copy the sentence on the lines.

1. <u>Neighbors found her lying on the ground, unconscious.</u>

2. _____

3. _____

4. _____

5. _____

6. _____

_____

_____

7. _____

_____

_____

8. _____

_____

_____

9. _____

_____

_____

UNDERSTANDING CAUSE AND EFFECT

Find the best way to complete each sentence. Write the letter of your answer on the line.

1. Pamela fell to the ground __c__

2. It was not easy for Pamela to adjust to being blind _____

3. Pamela called Mitch _____

4. Mitch thought Pamela wouldn't love him _____

5. Pamela thought Mitch wouldn't love her _____

a. because she was single and lived alone.

b. because he wasn't handsome.

c. because she had had a stroke.

d. because she was blind.

e. because the drain in her sink was clogged.

4 DISCUSSION

Mitch thought Pamela wouldn't love him because he wasn't handsome. How important is it to be handsome or beautiful?

A Work as a class to make a list of qualities that are important when you are looking for a husband, wife, boyfriend, or girlfriend. Your teacher will write your list on the board. For example:

good-looking
honest
hardworking

B Choose two qualities that are very important to you and two that are not important. Write those qualities in the chart below. Then compare your answers with a classmate's.

Very Important	Not Important

C Form groups with only men or only women in them. The women's groups make a list of the four qualities they think are most important when choosing a husband, and the men's groups make a list of the four qualities they think are most important when choosing a wife.

Four Most Important Qualities When Choosing a Wife/Husband
1.
2.
3.
4.

D Each group shares its list with the whole class. How different are the men's and women's lists?

E Discuss the importance of physical appearance in the United States. In small groups, read the following statements. Check (✓) *TRUE* if you think the statement is true and *FALSE* if you think the statement is false. Report your group's answers to the whole class.

	TRUE	FALSE
1. In political elections, the better-looking candidate usually wins.	☐	☐
2. In presidential elections, the taller candidate usually wins.	☐	☐
3. Tall people make more money than short people.	☐	☐
4. Attractive people make more money than unattractive people.	☐	☐
5. Teachers think attractive students are smarter than unattractive students.	☐	☐
6. People usually marry people who are as good-looking as they are.	☐	☐
7. Babies look at the faces of attractive people longer than they look at the faces of unattractive people.	☐	☐
8. Attractive people who have a problem get more help than unattractive people.	☐	☐

F Now check the Key on page 138 to see if you guessed correctly.

5 WRITING

After Mitch fixed Pamela's sink, Pamela made some tea and they sat at her kitchen table and talked.

A What do men and women talk about when they're getting to know each other? Work as a class to make three lists. Your teacher will write your lists on the board.

1. Topics that men talk about when they are with other men

2. Topics that women talk about when they are with other women

3. Topics for a man and woman to talk about when they are together

B Work with a partner and choose one of the following writing activities.

1. Write a conversation between a man and woman when they first meet. The woman should speak six to eight times, and the man should speak six to eight times.

2. Write Pamela and Mitch's first conversation. Pamela should speak six to eight times, and Mitch should speak six to eight times.

C Practice the conversation with your partner. If you would like to, read it in front of the class.

CHALLENGE

Pamela and Mitch both believed there were obstacles to their love: Pamela thought Mitch wouldn't love her because she was blind, and Mitch thought Pamela wouldn't love him because he wasn't handsome. In the end, it turned out that these were not real obstacles at all.

The couples in the following three stories faced obstacles to their love, too. But their obstacles were real.

A | **Read how each love story began.**

1 | Elizabeth and Robert

When Elizabeth met Robert in 1845, she was a famous poet in England and nearly 40 years old. Robert, 34, was also a poet, but not a famous one. They met after Robert wrote her what was essentially a fan letter. "I love your verses with all my heart," he wrote. Elizabeth wrote back, and Robert asked to meet her. During the next year, they wrote over 500 love letters to each other.

Robert wanted to marry Elizabeth and move to a warm, sunny climate. She had a chronic cough that was the result of a childhood lung infection, and he feared that one more winter in England could kill her.

Because of her poor health, Elizabeth had spent most of her life at home with her father. He opposed her marriage; he wanted her to stay with him. "Can't you see that Robert's a fortune hunter?" he asked Elizabeth. "He doesn't want you—he wants your fame."

2 | June and Johnny

Johnny was in love with June, and she was in love with him. But she was afraid to get involved with him. Johnny had many wonderful qualities, including enormous talent. And they had common interests—they were both singers and songwriters. In fact, they met while performing together. But Johnny was addicted to drugs.

His addiction began with one little pill he took to give him energy while on a concert tour in the late 1950s. Gradually, his drug use increased; he was in jail eight times because of the drugs. After seven years of drug abuse, Johnny decided to stop. He asked June for help, and she talked to her father about it. "Let's pack our suitcases," her father said. "Your mother and I will help, too."

June and her parents went to Johnny's house and searched his bedroom for pills, which they threw away. Then Johnny went into the bedroom, and they locked the door. He stayed there for three days. The three days without drugs broke his addiction for a while. But during the next few years, he had several relapses into drug use. He finally gave up drugs for good after a six-week stay at a drug rehabilitation center.

3 Anna and Boris

Anna and Boris had been married for less than a week when Anna disappeared. They got married in their village in Siberia on a Saturday morning in 1946. The following Tuesday, Boris went to a neighboring village to work for a few days. When he returned, Anna was gone. Neighbors told him that soldiers had taken Anna and her entire family away. Her father had been critical of Stalin, the country's leader. That was a crime, and he and his family were exiled to a faraway village.

Frantic, Boris went from village to village for months looking for Anna. He couldn't find her. Meanwhile, Anna's mother was telling her she had to forget Boris. "You can never go home," her mother told her, "and Boris will never find you here. You're still young. You can be happy with someone else." Eventually, Anna did marry someone else. Boris did, too. But he never forgot Anna, his first love. And Anna never forgot him.

B What were the obstacles the couples in the stories faced? Write the number of the story on the line.

_____ a. The government separated them because of her father's political views.

_____ b. Her father opposed their marriage.

_____ c. He was addicted to drugs.

C How do you think the stories ended? Read the endings below. Match each ending with a story. Write the number of the story on the line.

_____ a. One evening, when they were singing together in a concert, he turned to her and asked, "Will you marry me?" She didn't say anything, so he repeated the question: "Will you marry me?" There were 7,000 people in the audience, and they began to chant, "Say yes! Say yes!" "All right," she answered. "Yes, I will." They were married for 35 years. They died in 2003 within four months of each other.

_____ b. They didn't see each other for the next 60 years. When they were over 80 years old, after their spouses had died, they both returned to the village where they had met and married. She wanted to see the house where they had lived together for only three days. He had come to visit his parents' graves. She was standing in front of the house when she noticed an old man looking at her. "Is it you?" he asked. Incredibly, they were both in the village on the same day. A few weeks later, they remarried.

_____ c. They married in secret. After the wedding, she returned to her father's house for a week. Then the couple moved to Italy. Her health improved there, and three years later, she gave birth to a son. Both continued to write poetry, and he, too, became famous. While in Italy, she wrote a poem to her husband that became one of the best-known love poems in the English language. It begins, "How do I love thee[1]? Let me count the ways." She died in her husband's arms at age 55.

D Look at the Key on page 138 to see the full names of the couples in the three stories.

E Do you know a couple who faced an obstacle to their love? Tell the class about them.

---

1 *Thee* is an old form of the word *you*.

UNIT 2

Simeulue Island

1 PRE-READING

What do you know about the tsunami of 2004? Share what you know with the class. Your teacher will write the information on the board and organize it in an idea map. See below how one class began their idea map.

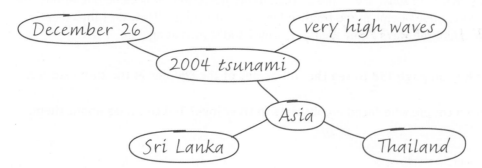

December 26

very high waves

2004 tsunami

Asia

Sri Lanka

Thailand

The *Semong* (The Tsunami)

On the island of Simeulue in Indonesia, an old woman was telling a story to her grandchildren. "Once upon a time," she began, "there was a little girl named Kiro. Kiro lived in our village a long time ago—before you were born, before your parents were born, even before I was born. One day Kiro was in her house, helping her mother in the kitchen. Suddenly the ground began to shake. It shook and shook. It shook so hard that Kiro and her mother couldn't stand up, and they fell to the floor. All around them, dishes and pots were falling from the shelves and crashing to the floor. Finally, the shaking stopped. Kiro and her mother got up and walked out of their house."

"Then what happened, Grandma?" the children asked, although they knew what happened next. They had heard the story many times before.

"Kiro looked toward the beach," the grandmother continued, "and she saw something she had never seen before. All the water was leaving the beach. It was going out toward the sea. Where there once had been a narrow beach, there was a wide beach. Beautiful, colorful fish were lying all over the beach. Some people were picking up the fish and putting them in baskets. Other people were standing on the beach looking out at the water. But Kiro remembered the story her grandmother had told her. So she yelled to the people."

Here the grandmother paused. "Do you remember what Kiro yelled?" she asked her grandchildren.

"Run!" the children answered.

"That's right. Kiro yelled, 'Run! *Semong*!' Do you remember what a *semong* is?"

"A big wave!" the children answered.

"Yes," the old woman said. "A very big wave. Bigger than a boy. Bigger than a girl. Bigger than a house. Bigger than a palm tree."

She continued the story.

"'Run! *Semong*!' Kiro yelled. People put down their baskets of fish. They picked up their children. They ran to the hills behind our village. Then the *semong* came. A wall of water came toward the village. The water covered the beach and covered the houses and covered the trees. But all the people were safe because they were standing on the hills. And that is the story of Kiro and the *semong*."

Why was the old woman telling her grandchildren this story? She was warning them. In 1907, a tsunami—a giant wave—had hit their island, and many people had died. She wanted the children to be ready if another tsunami came.

Another tsunami did come to Simeulue. On the morning of December 26, 2004, an earthquake in the Indian Ocean created huge waves. The waves came first to Simeulue, the island closest to the earthquake.

A 33-year-old man named Suhardin, who lives on the coast of Simeulue, told a reporter about his experience. He said his grandmother had told him stories about the *semong*. But he didn't think about his grandmother's stories when he felt the earthquake. Nothing had happened after an earthquake three years ago. Why would there be a *semong* after this earthquake? But then a man ran past him yelling, "Semong! Semong!" Suhardin thought about his grandmother and decided to climb one of the hills behind his village.

When he got to the top of the hill, hundreds of people were already there, and more people were climbing the steep hill. Some were helping old people up the hill, and some were carrying small children. Before long, everyone in the village was on top of the hill, looking out toward the sea. For thirty minutes, nothing happened. Then, just as Suhardin was thinking about walking back down the hill, the water along the coast rushed out to the sea. After that, the first wave came: A wall of water over 30 feet (10 meters) high crashed on the shore below. Suhardin watched the water take his whole village out to sea.

The tsunami of 2004 hit fourteen countries, and more than 280,000 people died. But on the island of Simeulue, with 75,000 people, only seven died. Why did so many people on Simeulue survive?

They survived for two reasons. First, they survived because Simeulue's hills are close to the

continued ▶

coast. When the tsunami came, people could run to safety. People in other places were not so lucky; they had no nearby hills to run to. Second, they survived because they remembered the stories the old people told about the *semong*, stories that warned them to run to the hills after an earthquake.

The people of Simeulue hope another tsunami never comes to their island. But just in case, they will tell their grandchildren the story of the *semong*. Someday the story could save their grandchildren's lives, just as the story saved theirs.

2 VOCABULARY

LOOKING AT THE STORY

Complete the sentences with the words below.

coast	island	survived	whole
crashed	paused	village	wide
huge	steep	warn	yelled

1. There is water all around Simeulue. It is an _____island_____.

2. Only 500 people lived in Kiro's _____.

3. The dishes and pots made a loud noise when they _____ to the floor.

4. The beach near Kiro's village was narrow, but after the water left, it was _____.

5. Kiro's grandmother stopped in her story because she wanted to be sure the children understood the word *semong*. She _____ for a minute and asked them, "Do you remember what a *semong* is?"

6. Everyone on the beach heard Kiro because she spoke loudly. "Run!" she _____.

7. The grandmother wanted the children to be ready if another dangerous tsunami came. She wanted to _____ them.

8. The first wave was over 30 feet (10 meters) high. It was _____.

9. Suhardin didn't live in the center of the island; he lived close to the water, on the _____.

10. It was difficult for old people and children to climb the hill behind Suhardin's village because the hill was _____.

11. The water covered everything in Suhardin's village—houses and shops, bicycles and cars. The water took the _____ village out to sea.

12. Simeulue had 75,000 people. Seven people died, and 74,993 _____.

LOOKING AT A NEW CONTEXT

A Choose five words from the list of words on page 14 that you want to remember. Use each word in your own sentence. Write your sentences on the lines below. Here, for example, is a sentence one student wrote using the word *huge*.

I saw a huge bear at the zoo.

1. _____

2. _____

3. _____

4. _____

5. _____

B Test your memory of the new words: Cross out the five words so that you can't read them. For example:

I saw a ~~huge~~ bear at the zoo.

C When you are finished with the exercises in this unit, come back to this exercise. Can you remember the words you crossed out?

D Sometimes you can write a word in a way that helps you remember it. Choose one of these words from the story: *crash, huge, island, pause, steep*. Write it in the box below in a way that helps you remember it. For example, you can write the word *wide* this way:

W I D E

E Now write your word in the same way on the board and share your idea with the class.

The *Semong* (The Tsunami)   **15**

3 COMPREHENSION/READING SKILLS

UNDERSTANDING THE MAIN IDEA

Imagine this: You and a friend are looking at the map below. How would you explain to your friend why almost everyone on the island of Simeulue survived? Write your explanation on the lines.

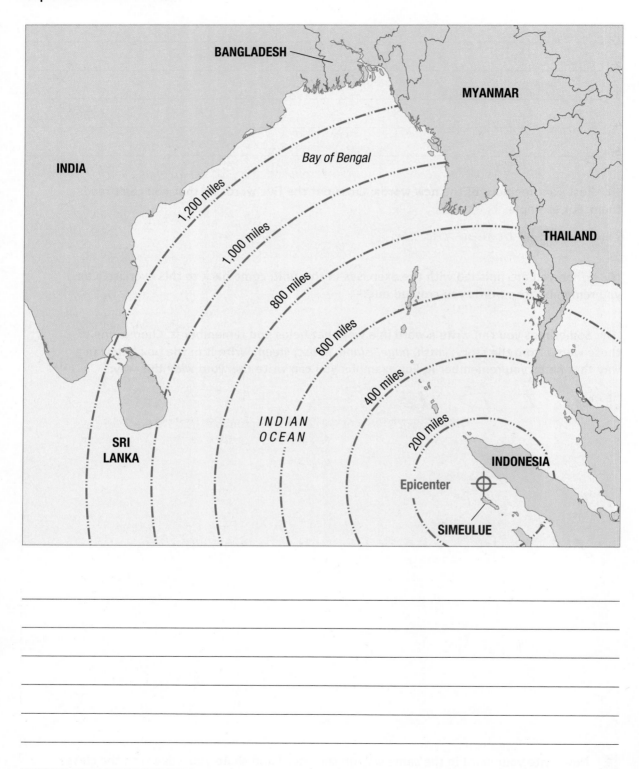

_____

_____

_____

_____

_____

_____

_____

UNDERSTANDING DETAILS

A Read the sentences with information from the story. One word in each sentence is not correct. Find the word and cross it out. Write the correct word.

Indonesia

1. The old woman in the story lived on an island in ~~Thailand~~.

2. She told her grandchildren a story about a girl named Sinta.

3. In 1950, a tsunami killed many people in Simeulue.

4. The 2004 earthquake was on the morning of January 26.

5. An earthquake in the Pacific Ocean created huge waves.

B Now write three sentences with information from the story, but change one word in each sentence so that the information is not correct.

6. _____

_____

7. _____

_____

8. _____

_____

C Give your sentences to a classmate. Your classmate will find the incorrect word in each sentence, cross it out, and write the correct word. When your classmate is finished, check the corrections.

RETELLING A STORY

Imagine this: It is many years from now. Suhardin, the man in the story, is an old man with grandchildren. Like the grandmother at the beginning of the story, Suhardin wants to warn his grandchildren. He tells them about his 2004 tsunami experience. Complete his story on your own paper. Write the story in words a child could understand.

When I was a little boy, my grandmother told me stories about the semong. "If there is an earthquake," my grandmother told me, "run to the hills!" But when I felt the earthquake in 2004, I didn't think about my grandmother's stories. I didn't run. But then a man ran past me. He was yelling, . . .

4 DISCUSSION

A Work as a class to make a list of natural disasters (for example, tsunamis and hurricanes). Your teacher will write your list on the board.

B Copy the words in the spaces along the top of the chart below. On the left side of the chart, write the names of your classmates' countries.

Country	tsunamis	hurricanes						

C Walk around the room and find a person from each country. Ask your classmates if the natural disasters written at the top of the chart happen in their countries. Check (✓) your classmates' "yes" answers.

D Ask your classmates for more information about their "yes" answers.

5 WRITING

The old woman told a story to warn her grandchildren about a tsunami. All over the world, people tell stories that warn of danger or teach a lesson.

A   Write a story that warns of danger or teaches a lesson. It can be a story that people in your country tell, a story from your personal life, or a story that you made up. Here is what one student wrote.

When I lived in California, there were earthquakes sometimes. One day when there was an earthquake, my friend was at home with her baby. She ran to the baby's bed, picked up the baby, and ran to a doorway. She stood in the doorway and held the baby. A piece of the ceiling fell down on the baby's bed. So if there is an earthquake, stand in a doorway.

B   Have you ever experienced a natural disaster? Write about your experience. Here is what one student wrote.

Costa Rica is a small country, but it has eight volcanoes. Currently three of them are active, so we have many earthquakes.

I remember one (among many) really well because my brother Eduardo was visiting us then. We lived in a second-floor apartment with wood floors. Eduardo is a big man, and when he walked across the floor, the floor made a noise. I told him three times, "Eduardo, don't make so much noise when you walk. It bothers the people living below us." He told me, "I'm not making noise." Then we realized an earthquake was causing the floor to make noise. A few minutes later, we had a much stronger earthquake, and everything started shaking and falling down.

When the earthquake was over, my brother said, "Let's go see the damage the earthquake did." I told him, "Eduardo, let's not go because we might have another earthquake." But he insisted, so we went. When we walked through the streets, we saw many signs and cables on the ground. The walls of some buildings had fallen down. A man told us that he had been ready to get into his car when the earthquake happened and the wall of a building fell down on it.

Days later, friends told me that they had been in a supermarket and could hear glass breaking as jars of food crashed to the floor.

That earthquake caused a lot of damage.

CHALLENGE

Many popular vacation spots are in the area hit by the 2004 tsunami, so some of the people who experienced it were tourists. The following are three stories of people who were on vacation when the tsunami hit. They are first-person accounts—that is, the people told the stories in their own words.

A Read the stories.

1 Jillian Searle

Home country: Australia
Age: 32 (in 2004)
Occupation: Homemaker

My husband and I were on vacation in Phuket, Thailand,[1] with our two sons: Lachie, who was five, and Blake, who was two. We were all relaxing at the hotel pool. My husband had just left—he'd gone back up to our room to get some clothes for Blake. I saw a big wall of water coming straight for us, and I just started running. I had both my boys in my arms, one in each arm, and we started going under. I knew that if I held on to both, we would all die. I just thought I'd better let go of Lachie, the oldest. He was squeezing me and saying, "Don't let go of me,

Mummy." I saw a teenage girl nearby. "Grab him!" I screamed to her as I let go of Lachie's hand. She grabbed hold of him for a moment, but she had to let go because she was going under. And then I couldn't see Lachie.

After the water receded, my husband and I looked for Lachie. I was screaming trying to find him. We thought he was dead. I remember telling my husband, "There is no way I can live my life knowing that I took his hand off mine." We looked for about two hours, and then we found him with a hotel security guard. He'd kept his head above water by holding onto a door in the hotel lobby.

We are so lucky. I'm just thankful I still have my two kids with me.

2 Stephen Boulton

Home country: Scotland
Age: 34 (in 2004)
Occupation: Plumber and volunteer firefighter

I was celebrating my 34th birthday with my wife and three children—they were 12, 4, and 2—at a resort in the Maldives.[2] We were on the pier when suddenly the tide came in. Before we knew it, the water was up to our chests. It was so strong that we knew if we fell, it would pull us under. My wife and I grabbed our kids and waded through horrendous currents back to our hotel. When we turned around to look at the pier, we saw that it was gone.

After about five minutes, the tide went back

out as far as you could see, as if someone pulled the plug. I didn't like what I was seeing. We climbed up a palm tree with the younger kids on our backs. I tied each child to a branch of the tree with beach towels. Then the second wave came. It was like the whole sea was heading our way. It sped past within inches of our feet. After the water receded, I climbed down to help the injured, but my family stayed up in the tree for a couple of hours, just to be on the safe side.

I never thought for a second we wouldn't be OK. From the moment it all started going crazy, I worked out every possible scenario—and solutions. That's just the way I am.

---

1 Phuket Island is off the west coast of Thailand. It is 310 miles (500 kilometers) from the epicenter of the earthquake.

2 The Republic of Maldives is an island nation southwest of India. It consists of 1,192 islands, 200 of which are inhabited. It is 1,400 miles (2,252 kilometers) west of the epicenter of the earthquake.

3 Tilly Smith

Home country: England
Age: 10 (in 2004)
Occupation: Student

I was on holiday with my parents and little sister in Phuket, Thailand. We were on the beach, and the water started to go funny. There were bubbles, and then the tide went out all of a sudden. I recognized what was happening and had a feeling there was going to be a tsunami. Just two weeks before, our geography teacher had taught us about earthquakes and how they cause tsunamis.

He told us that after the sea sucked backwards, a tsunami would come in five or ten minutes. When the water went back, I said, "Mummy, we must get off the beach *now*." My mum wanted to look at what was going on, but when I told her about tsunamis, she had second thoughts. We ran off the beach as fast as we could. My parents warned the other people on the beach—there were about 100 people there—and they all ran, too. We went up to the third floor of our hotel. A few minutes later, the tsunami came. After the wave came, I said to Mummy, "I told you."

B Look at the photos. They illustrate scenes in the stories. Which photo goes best with which story? Write the number of the story on the line below the photo.

a. _____

b. _____

c. _____

C Read the newspaper headlines. Which headline goes with which story? Write the number of the story next to the correct headline.

_____ Family Saved by Their Towels

_____ Geography Lesson Saves Family

_____ Which Child to Save?

1 PRE-READING

Compare gestures in your native country with gestures in other countries. Your teacher will ask you the questions below. Answer the questions using only your hands, arms, and head. Don't speak! As you answer each question, look at your classmates. Which gestures are the same? Which gestures are different?

What gesture do you use for . . . ?

1. "Come here."
2. "Go away."
3. "Stop."
4. "Please be quiet."
5. "I can't hear you."
6. "I'll call you."
7. "Who, me?"

8. "Yes."
9. "No."
10. "Maybe."
11. "I don't know."
12. "Wait a minute."
13. "He or she's crazy."
14. "He or she's intelligent."

15. "Money."
16. "A long time ago."
17. "This is good."
18. "This is bad."
19. "This is so-so—not bad, but not good."
20. "This is delicious."

More Alike Than Different

Everyone listened attentively as the woman spoke.

"If you want to say 'OK,' don't make a circle with your thumb and first finger," the woman began. "That means OK here in the United States, but in Russia it's an obscene gesture."

The audience of 300 Americans chuckled; a few people took notes.

"It's all right to admire something," the woman continued, "but don't be too enthusiastic. Don't say, 'I *really* like your tablecloth.' Your Russian friend will offer you the tablecloth and will be offended if you don't take it."

"When Russians have a conversation, they usually stand closer together than Americans do," the woman said. "Try not to step back when you're talking to a Russian. Your Russian friend will think you're trying to leave."

"And one more thing: Don't worry if Russians don't always smile at you when you smile at them. It doesn't mean that you aren't welcome in Russia. People there usually don't smile at strangers."

The woman was preparing the Americans for their trip to Russia. In Russia, the language, customs, and food would be different. The Americans wanted to learn about these differences before their trip. They didn't want to experience culture shock.

When they arrived in Russia, the Americans were glad that they had prepared for their trip. Most of them experienced only a little culture shock. They enjoyed their visit and made a lot of Russian friends.

Making friends was, in fact, the purpose of the trip. It was planned by Friendship Force International, an organization that promotes world peace. Friendship Force International believes that people who are friends will not fight wars. So, to help people from all over the world become friends, it organizes exchanges of people. It has sent more than a half million people to live with families in other countries for a week or two. The U.S.-Russian exchange was one of the largest exchanges it has ever organized. Friendship Force sent 300 Americans to Russia and 300 Russians to the United States.

The Russians, like the Americans, prepared for their visit by learning about life in the other country. Still, they too experienced a little culture shock.

The Russians were surprised at the differences between everyday life in the United States and Russia. For example, Americans usually don't take off their shoes when they enter a home; Russians usually do. Most Americans drink unfiltered water from a kitchen faucet; most Russians don't. Americans often answer the question *How are you?* with one word: *Fine*. And Russians? They often answer that question with a story!

The Russians knew that Americans liked to eat fast food in restaurants, but they were disappointed to see that Americans ate fast meals at home, too. In Russia, the evening meal often lasts an hour or two because families sit at the table and talk. When American families eat together—*if* they eat together—they often eat quickly and don't take time for long conversations. "Why don't American families spend more time together?" the Russians wondered.

They wondered about something else, too: "Why do strangers smile at us? Are we doing something funny?" They thought it was odd.

In spite of their differences in language and culture, the Russians and Americans became friends. In fact, most people who go on Friendship Force trips make friends, no matter where they go.

Perhaps an 11-year-old girl summarized the Friendship Force experience best. She and some children from her school traveled to Russia with the American group. When they returned to the United States, their teacher asked them to write about their trip. She wrote, "I have learned a lot from this experience. I learned to adapt to a different culture. And I learned that people all over the world are more alike than they are different."

2 VOCABULARY

LOOKING AT THE STORY

Read the following sentences. Then complete the statements about the words in *italics*. Circle the letter of the correct answer.

Everyone listened *attentively* as the woman spoke.

1. To listen attentively is to listen _____.
   a. carefully
   b. nervously

"Don't make a circle with your thumb and first finger," the woman said. "That's an *obscene* gesture in Russia." *The audience* of 300 Americans *chuckled*.

2. An obscene gesture is _____.
   a. not polite
   b. polite

3. An audience _____.
   a. listens or watches
   b. sings, dances, or speaks

4. To chuckle is to _____.
   a. sing loudly
   b. laugh quietly

"It's all right to *admire* something," the woman said, "but don't be too *enthusiastic*. Don't say, 'I really like your tablecloth.' Your Russian friend will offer you the tablecloth and will be *offended* if you don't take it."

5. If you admire something, you _____.
   a. don't like it
   b. like it

6. If you are enthusiastic, you are _____.
   a. interested and excited
   b. bored and tired

7. People who are offended are _____.
   a. a little angry because their feelings are hurt
   b. a little nervous because they don't know what to do

The Russians knew that Americans liked to eat fast food in restaurants, but they were *disappointed* to see that Americans ate fast meals at home, too.

8. People who are disappointed are _____.
   a. not happy
   b. happy

The Russians *wondered* about something else, too: "Why do strangers smile at us? Are we doing something funny?" They thought it was *odd*.

9. If you wonder about something, you are _____.
   a. worried about it and afraid to hear more
   b. thinking about it and interested in knowing more

10. Something that is odd is _____.
    a. unusual
    b. serious

An 11-year-old girl wrote, "I learned to *adapt* to a different culture. And I learned that people all over the world are more *alike* than they are different."

11. People who adapt _____.
   a. don't change   b. change

12. *Alike* means _____.
   a. the same   b. strange

LOOKING AT A NEW CONTEXT

A **Complete the sentences to show that you understand the meanings of the new words.**

1. Someone I really admire is _____.

2. Someone or something that makes me chuckle is _____.

3. People who immigrate to the United States probably find it difficult to adapt to _____

_____.

4. People who immigrate to the United States probably find it easy to adapt to _____

_____.

5. I would listen attentively if someone were talking about _____.

6. I would be disappointed if someone gave me _____ for my birthday.

7. I would be enthusiastic if someone invited me to _____.

8. I often wonder about _____.

9. I think it is odd when people _____.

B **In small groups, take turns reading your sentences aloud. Ask your classmates questions about their sentences.**

3 COMPREHENSION / READING SKILLS

UNDERSTANDING THE MAIN IDEAS

Circle the letter of the best answer.

1. "More Alike Than Different" is about _____.
   a. gestures that are used all over the world
   b. a U.S.-Russian exchange of people that was organized by Friendship Force International
   c. the difficulties of international travel

2. Friendship Force International is _____.
   a. an international organization that promotes world peace
   b. an organization that prepares Americans for visiting Russia
   c. an international organization of children who visit other countries

3. Friendship Force International believes that _____.
   a. families should spend more time together
   b. people who are friends won't fight wars
   c. people who don't speak English will experience culture shock in the United States

4. To help people become friends, Friendship Force International _____.
   a. sends language teachers all over the world
   b. gives people free airplane tickets
   c. organizes exchanges of people

5. The Americans prepared for their visit by _____.
   a. experiencing culture shock
   b. writing essays
   c. learning about Russian life

6. Before their trip, the Americans got information about _____.
   a. museums in Russia
   b. customs in Russia
   c. public transportation in Russia

7. The Russians were surprised at the differences between _____.
   a. the political systems in the United States and Russia
   b. universities in the United States and Russia
   c. everyday life in the United States and Russia

8. Although their languages and cultures were different, the Russians and the Americans _____.
   a. ate the same food
   b. became friends
   c. had the same everyday lives

UNDERSTANDING SUPPORTING DETAILS

Read each sentence on the left. Which sentence on the right gives you more details? Write the letter of the answer on the line.

_c_ 1. It's all right to admire something, but don't be too enthusiastic.

_____ 2. In Russia, the way people have conversations is different.

_____ 3. The Russians were surprised when they saw Americans enter a home.

_____ 4. Friendship Force International organizes exchanges of people.

_____ 5. Schoolchildren traveled to Russia with the American group.

a. They usually didn't take off their shoes.

b. Their teacher asked them to write about their trip.

c. Don't say, "I *really* like your tablecloth."

d. Russians stand closer together.

e. It has sent more than half a million people to live with families in other countries.

4 DISCUSSION

The people in the story learned a lot about another culture.

A Interview a classmate from another country. Ask your classmate the questions below about everyday life in your classmate's country.

1. If a guest sees something in your home and says, "I *really* like it," do you say, "Please—take it"?

2. How far apart do people stand when they talk? Could you show me, please?

3. Do strangers smile at one another?

4. Do people take off their shoes when they enter a home?

5. Do people drink unfiltered water from a kitchen faucet?

6. How do people answer the question *How are you*? Do they answer with a word, or do they answer with a story?

7. Do people like to eat fast food in restaurants?

8. How long does the evening meal last?

B Tell the class what you learned about the culture of your classmate's country.

5 WRITING

A Imagine this: Friendship Force International is sending a group of people to your native country. What might surprise the visitors? Write a paragraph to prepare the visitors so that they don't experience culture shock. Here is what one student wrote.

If you go to a town in Mexico when there is a festival, be prepared to eat a lot! If you and your hosts go from house to house to visit friends and family, they will want to give you food. If you say, "I just ate. I'm full," they will make a plate of food for you anyway. If you say, "No, no, I'm really full," they will say, "Oh, that's fine! Take it with you!" They will put the food in a little container so you can take it home. You must take something with you. You cannot leave without taking food.

B Are you living in another country? Imagine that friends or relatives from your country are coming to visit. What might surprise them? Write them a letter. Prepare them so that they don't experience culture shock.

CHALLENGE

Test your knowledge of other cultures and customs. Imagine this: You are traveling around the world and you find yourself in the following situations.

A **Read about each situation. Then answer the question, circling the letter of the best answer.**

1

You are visiting a temple in Thailand. In the courtyard of the temple, people are sitting on the ground. They are resting and talking. You are tired, so you sit down on the ground, too. You lean back on the temple wall and stretch your feet out in front of you. The Thai people frown at you. You know you are doing something wrong. What is it?

a. Only Thai people sit on the ground at temples. People from other countries should stand or sit on a chair.

b. Your back is against the wall of the temple. It is against the law to touch any part of a temple in Thailand.

c. You are sitting with your feet stretched out in front of you. That means you are pointing your feet at people. It is very impolite.

2

You get on a city bus in Korea. The bus is crowded, and there are no empty seats. So you stand. You are holding a big package. A woman who is sitting near you pulls at your package. What should you do?

a. The woman is trying to tell you that it is illegal to get on a crowded bus with a big package. Get off the bus at the next stop and take a taxi.

b. The woman wants to help you. Give her your package and smile.

c. Thieves are common on crowded city buses. Hold on to your package tightly.

3

You are shopping in France. You are carrying a shopping bag full of things you bought at a department store. You walk into a small shop and look around. You don't see anything you want, so you leave. As you are leaving, you see that the shop owner is frowning at you. What have you done wrong?

a. You carried your shopping bag around the small shop. You should have given it to the shop owner to hold for you.

b. You were impolite. You didn't say, "Bonjour," when you entered the shop, and you didn't say, "Au revoir," when you left.

c. You didn't buy anything. You should have bought something small, just to be polite.

4

You are at a tea shop in Nepal. The man next to you—a Nepali—pays ten rupees for his cup of tea and leaves. When you get up to leave, the shop owner tells you the price of your cup of tea is thirty rupees. What do you do?

a. Be firm. Tell the shop owner you saw the other man pay only ten rupees. Say that you'll pay only ten rupees, too.

b. Try to bargain the price down to at least fifteen rupees.

c. Ask again how much the tea is. If the shop owner says thirty rupees again, pay the thirty rupees.

5

You are studying at a university in the United States. In line at the cafeteria, you meet a friendly American student. You have a long conversation. You are new in the United States and lonely; you hope that you and the student can be friends. You exchange phone numbers, but your new friend doesn't call you. A week later, you see her again in the cafeteria. She smiles and says, "Hi," but she passes by your table to sit with some friends. What should you do?

a. Walk over to her table. Ask her, "Why didn't you call me?"

b. Forget her. She probably doesn't want to make new friends.

c. Call her once or twice. Invite her to do something together. If she always says she is busy, then forget her.

6

You are living in Spain. You have to sign a paper in the presence of a notary public. So, you make an appointment with a notary public for 10:00 a.m. When you arrive at 10:00, a receptionist politely asks you to take a seat. At 11:30, you are still waiting for the notary. What should you do?

a. Tell the receptionist that you can't wait any longer. Ask her to take you to the notary public's office immediately.

b. Walk past the receptionist and knock on the notary public's door.

c. Keep quiet and keep waiting.

7

At a party in France, you are introduced to a stranger. What is a good question to begin a conversation?

a. "Are you married?"

b. "What kind of work do you do?"

c. "Have you seen the new Monet exhibit at the Musée d'Orsay?"

8

You have just moved to the United States. You want cable and high-speed Internet access installed in your apartment as soon as possible. What should you do?

a. Call the cable company. Take the first appointment that is available.

b. Go to the cable company. Explain how important it is for you to get Internet access as soon as possible.

c. Ask people if they know anyone who works at the cable company. When you have the name of a cable company employee, call the employee. Ask him/her to move your name to the top of the list.

9

You are living in Malaysia. You have a puppy. You have invited a Malaysian family, who is Muslim, to your house. What should you do about your puppy?

a. Put the puppy in another room, out of sight.

b. Invite your Malaysian guests to play with the puppy.

c. Be sure to tell your Malaysian guests that the puppy doesn't bite.

10

You are living in Italy. An Italian family invites you to visit them at 4:00 p.m. Two hours later, you and the family are still laughing and talking. They invite you to stay for dinner. You have no plans for dinner. You should say,

a. "Yes, thank you," and stay.

b. "Yes, thank you, but only if I can help make dinner."

c. "Thank you, but I can't tonight. Let's get together for dinner another time."

B Check the Key on page 138 to find out the correct answers.

UNIT 4

1 PRE-READING

Just for fun, test your knowledge of acupuncture. Read the statements below. If you think the statement is true, check (✓) TRUE. If you think the statement is false, check (✓) FALSE. If you aren't sure, take a guess.

	TRUE	FALSE
1. Acupuncture for goldfish is common in Asia.	☐	☐
2. A doctor who uses acupuncture is an acupractor.	☐	☐
3. All acupuncture needles are 1 inch (2.5 centimeters) long.	☐	☐
4. Acupuncture is very painful.	☐	☐
5. Acupuncture needles must stay in place for two hours.	☐	☐
6. Acupuncture needles always go in the place where the patient has pain.	☐	☐
7. The Japanese were the first to use acupuncture.	☐	☐

Now check the Key on page 138 to see if you guessed correctly.

Healthy Again

Mr. Cho was worried. Something was wrong with his goldfish. They had red patches on their skin, they weren't eating, and they didn't have much energy. Mr. Cho thought the fish probably had an infection. To cure the infection, he stuck needles into the backs of the fish. That may seem unusual to some people, but it didn't seem unusual to Mr. Cho. Mr. Cho is an acupuncturist—a person who uses needles to treat illness and pain.

Mr. Cho left the needles in the fish for several minutes and then took them out. During the next few days, he repeated the treatments. Soon the fish began to feel better. They swam with more energy and started to eat again, and the red patches on their skin disappeared. Did the fish get better because of the acupuncture treatments? Mr. Cho thinks so.

Although acupuncture for goldfish is uncommon, acupuncture for people is very common in Asia. Acupuncturists there help people who have medical problems such as infections, backaches, and stomachaches. They even use acupuncture during operations so that patients won't feel pain.

To see what happens during an acupuncture treatment, let's imagine that Ming, a man who often has headaches, decides to go to Dr. Han, an acupuncturist. This is what might happen at Dr. Han's office:

First, Dr. Han examines Ming and asks him about his headaches. There are many kinds of headaches, and Dr. Han needs to know what kind of headaches Ming has.

Then Dr. Han decides where to insert the needles. Ming is surprised when Dr. Han tells him that she will insert needles in his neck and foot, but none in his head. That is not unusual. Often acupuncture needles are not inserted in the place where the patient feels pain.

Next, Dr. Han chooses the needles, which range in size from ½-inch (1.25 centimeters) long to 6 inches (15 centimeters). Dr. Han chooses 1-inch (2.5 centimeters) needles for Ming and begins to insert them. Ming feels a little pinch when each needle goes in. That is not unusual either. Some patients say it hurts a little when the needles go in; other patients say it doesn't hurt at all. The needles stay in place for fifteen minutes. Then Dr. Han removes them. Before he goes home, Ming makes an appointment to see Dr. Han in a week. Dr. Han says that Ming will know in a few weeks if the treatments are working.

Acupuncture has helped millions of people—not only in Asia, but all over the world. People say that acupuncture works. But *how* does it work?

One explanation of how acupuncture works is thousands of years old. The ancient Chinese, who were the first to use acupuncture, believed that energy flowed through the human body. They thought that sometimes too much energy—or too little energy—flowed to one part of the body. That caused pain or sickness. There were, however, several hundred places on the body where an acupuncturist could change the flow of energy. Those places were called acupuncture points. A needle inserted into an acupuncture point on a patient's leg, for example, changed the flow of energy to the patient's stomach. When the energy flowed correctly again, the patient would feel better.

There are also several modern explanations of how acupuncture works. Scientists point out that the acupuncture points have many more nerve endings than other places on the skin. Nerve endings receive pain messages when someone is sick or hurt. The pain messages then travel through the nerves. Perhaps acupuncture also sends messages through the nerves. These messages interrupt pain messages that are on their way to the brain. Because the pain messages never reach the brain, the patient feels better. Or perhaps the numb feeling some patients experience after acupuncture is simply the body's normal reaction to injury.

People who have been helped by acupuncture probably don't care which explanation is correct. They are just happy to be like Mr. Cho's fish—healthy again.

2 VOCABULARY

LOOKING AT THE STORY

Read each sentence. What is the meaning of the word(s) in *italics*? Circle the letter of the correct answer.

1. The fish had red *patches* on their skin.
   - (a.) places that looked different from the area around them
   - b. places where acupuncturists insert needles

2. Mr. Cho wanted to *cure the infection*.
   - a. learn about the fish
   - b. make the sickness go away

3. He *stuck* needles into the backs of the fish.
   - a. threw
   - b. pushed

4. An acupuncturist is a person who uses needles to *treat* illness and pain.
   - a. try to cure
   - b. cause

5. During the next few days, he *repeated the treatments*.
   - a. watched his fish very carefully
   - b. stuck needles into the backs of the fishes again

6. Acupuncture for fish is *uncommon*.
   - a. difficult
   - b. unusual

7. Dr. Han decides where to *insert* the needles.
   - a. put in
   - b. buy

8. The needles *range in size* from ½-inch long to 6 inches.
   - a. The shortest needles are ½-inch, the longest are 6 inches, and there are other sizes in between.
   - b. The needles come in two sizes: ½-inch and 6 inches.

9. The ancient Chinese believed that energy *flowed* through the human body.
   - a. escaped
   - b. traveled

10. These messages *interrupt* pain messages that are on their way to the brain.
    - a. stop
    - b. help

LOOKING AT SPECIAL EXPRESSIONS

Find the best way to complete each sentence. Write the letter of your answer on the line.

to point out = to draw attention to; to say, "Look at this." or "Think about this."

1. Scientists point out that acupuncture points _____
2. He pointed out that the bus we wanted to take _____
3. The students pointed out that the answers for Unit 9 _____

   a. arrived in Chicago in the middle of the night.

   b. were missing from the Answer Key.

   c. have many more nerve endings than other places on the skin.

3 COMPREHENSION/READING SKILLS

UNDERSTANDING THE MAIN IDEAS

What information is *not* in the story? Find the information and cross it out.

1. What was wrong with Mr. Cho's goldfish?
   a. They had red patches on their skin.
   b. They weren't eating.
   c. ~~They had fevers.~~
   d. They didn't have much energy.

2. To treat his fish, Dr. Cho
   a. stuck needles into their backs.
   b. left the needles in for several minutes.
   c. repeated the treatments during the next few days.
   d. gave them medicine.

3. After the acupuncture treatments, Mr. Cho's fish
   a. swam with more energy.
   b. started to eat again.
   c. were sold for a lot of money.
   d. didn't have red patches on their skin anymore.

4. Acupuncturists in Asia use acupuncture
   a. to help people with backaches.
   b. to treat broken bones.
   c. to help people with stomachaches.
   d. during operations so that patients don't feel pain.

5. What happened before Dr. Han inserted the needles?
   a. She told Ming how much the treatment would cost.
   b. She examined Ming and asked him about his headaches.
   c. She decided where to insert the needles.
   d. She chose 1-inch needles.

6. What happened during Ming's acupuncture treatment?
   a. Dr. Han inserted the needles.
   b. Ming felt a little pinch when each needle went in.
   c. Ming walked around the office.
   d. The needles stayed in place for fifteen minutes.

7. What are some explanations of how acupuncture works?
   a. It corrects the energy flow in the body.
   b. It interrupts pain messages on their way to the brain.
   c. It changes the flow of blood through the body.
   d. It causes tiny injuries that make the body feel numb.

UNDERSTANDING SUPPORTING DETAILS

Find the best way to complete each sentence. Write the letter of your answer on the line.

1. Something was wrong with Mr. Cho's goldfish. For example, _d_

2. The fish began to feel better. For example, _____

3. Acupuncture for people is very common in Asia. For example, _____

4. There are several hundred places on the body where an acupuncturist can change the flow of energy. For example, _____

a. acupuncturists there use acupuncture during operations so that patients don't feel pain.

b. a needle inserted into an acupuncture point on a patient's leg changes the flow of energy to the patient's stomach.

c. they swam with more energy and started to eat again.

d. they had red patches on their skin and they weren't eating.

4 DISCUSSION

Acupuncture is one type of medical treatment.

A Look at the following seven types of treatments for headaches. Read about the treatments. If you had headaches often, which treatments would you try? For each type of treatment, check (✓) *YES* or *NO*.

		YES	NO
1. Acupuncture	Insert one needle in the neck and another in the foot.	☐	☐
2. Acupressure (also called *Shiatsu*)	With your fingertips, push on the back of the head and the sides of the forehead. Massage the hand between the thumb and the first finger.	☐	☐
3. Chiropractic	Give a massage; move the bones in the spine so that the spine is straight.	☐	☐
4. Herbalism	Make tea by boiling a special plant or root. Give the tea to the patient, or give a pill made from the plant or root.	☐	☐
5. Holistic Health Care	Treat not only the headache, but also mental or emotional problems that could be causing the person's headache.	☐	☐
6. Spiritual Healing	Pray and put your hands on the person's forehead.	☐	☐
7. Traditional Western Medicine	Give painkillers.	☐	☐

B Work as a class and find out the answers to the following questions.

1. How many students would like to try acupuncture?

2. Which treatments would almost everyone in the class try?

3. Which treatments would almost no one try?

4. Has anyone in the class tried these types of medical treatments? What was the medical problem? Did the treatment work?

5 WRITING

Choose one of the following writing activities.

1. Write a letter to a friend who has a medical problem and is going to try acupuncture. Tell your friend what to expect during the treatment.

2. Write about a treatment that you have had for a medical problem. Describe the problem and the treatment.

_____

_____

_____

_____

_____

_____

_____

_____

_____

_____

_____

_____

_____

_____

_____

_____

_____

_____

_____

_____

_____

_____

_____

_____

_____

CHALLENGE

In Asia, acupuncture has been a common treatment for illness and pain for centuries. Recently acupuncture has become more common in the West. People are exchanging information about it on social media.

Read the three questions about acupuncture that people posted on social media. Each post is followed by two replies. If the reply is about a positive experience with acupuncture, circle the positive emoji. If the reply is about a disappointing experience with acupuncture, circle the disappointed emoji.

1

Marcus Williams

I just want to know if anyone has any suggestions because I am at the end of my rope! I have had the same headache for over a year now. I have been to countless neurologists, doctors, and chiropractors. I even went to a special headache clinic. Nothing has worked. Nothing showed up on the CT scan or MRI. All I want to do is get rid of the pain, even if it's just for a day. Should I try acupuncture?

Sara Davis I have a headache/acupuncture story—only it's not really mine, it happened to my mother-in-law. The acupuncturist told her to come in because she had a really bad headache. So she went in. The acupuncturist put some needles in and left. Then he came back and asked if she was feeling any better and she wasn't. He put more needles in and left. Well, he did this several more times—any better, no, more needles. In the meantime she was getting sicker and sicker (headache and stomachache). Finally, the last time he came back in, she said, "Oh, yes, it's much better" just to get those stupid needles out so she could go home and get her medicine. She said she never went back.

1. a. Circle one:

Tony Martinez I know acupuncture doesn't work for everyone, but it was a miracle for me. It did what five years of medications could not. I've been pain-free for six months now—no headaches. It's great and I'd go back in a minute if I even felt the slightest pain again.

1. b. Circle one:

Diana Parkinson

Tell me the truth.... Does acupuncture hurt? Even a little bit? How big are the needles, and what do they feel like?

afJones What acupuncture feels like: It sometimes feels like your skin is being pressed by the tip of a needle (but not puncturing the skin). It sometimes feels like someone has carefully slid a needle just under the very top layer of skin. (Or is it just me that feels that?) I can usually feel something, and sometimes something that I would go so far as to call pain. But it isn't at all severe, and in a way it's that sort of almost nice, tingly sort of pain. My acupuncturist doesn't go into details of what I'm feeling, but he does seem more pleased if I feel something than if I don't. :o) The needles are a couple of inches long, but only up to about ½ inch goes into the skin. Since starting acupuncture, I've come to learn that there is a route back to the "joy of life" I had before. Hope this helps.

2. a. Circle one:

sBrown It doesn't actually hurt, but I found it too stressful. When the needles went into my back, I felt my muscles, like, "paralyze." I was on my stomach in this horrid trapped position for 25 minutes. It was too hard for me, so I quit after five sessions. Afterward, I felt very relaxed, but during...argh!

2. b. Circle one:

3

Anna Lee

I'm a runner, and my knees are giving me trouble. Does anyone have experience with acupuncture for knee problems?

Matt Kasem My wife had a botched knee surgery that killed a lot of the nerve tissue in her left leg. She was lying in bed screaming and crying for months. We used painkillers, but they didn't help. So we went to an acupuncturist. The acupuncturist said it would cut the healing time in half, and it did. It was predicted that she would never walk normally again, and now she runs and goes hiking.

3. a. Circle one:

JJ Wilson My brother-in-law tried acupuncture for his bad knee (football injury), but he ended up having surgery anyway. Many people will tell you of their wonderful experiences with acupuncture. They'll also tell you that copper wristbands cure arthritis.

3. b. Circle one:

UNIT 5

Natalie Garibian

1 PRE-READING

A Read the statements and check your answers.

	YES	NO
1. I have relatives who live in a different country.	☐	☐
2. I have relatives who speak a language I don't understand.	☐	☐
3. My family has lost contact with some of our relatives.	☐	☐
4. My family sometimes talks about living relatives that I have never met.	☐	☐
5. I would like to meet relatives that I have never met.	☐	☐

B In a small group, tell your classmates more about your *YES* answers.

If You Have Time

Natalie Garibian was in her bedroom packing her suitcases. She was 20 years old, and she was both nervous and excited. The next day she was traveling from her home in Florida to Paris, France, where she would study for a semester. She was almost finished packing when her father walked into the room. He held two small black-and-white photos in his hand.

"When I was your age, I traveled, too," he said in Armenian, his native language. "I came to the United States. On the way, I stopped in Syria and stayed with a cousin for a few weeks. She and her husband had four children—a son and three daughters. They're the family in these photos. I heard from a relative that the daughters might be living in Paris now. I know you'll be busy in Paris. But I hope at some point you'll have time to look for these girls. I'd like to know how they are. And I'd like them to meet you."

Mr. Garibian turned the photos over and showed Natalie the names written on the back. "Of course, that was thirty years ago," he continued. "The girls are probably married and have different names. I'm sure they look very different, too. Maybe they don't even live in Paris. Still, I hope you have time to look for them."

Natalie took the photos from her father and sighed. "If I have time, Papa," Natalie answered in Armenian. "If I have time."

Natalie knew that she would have to study hard in Paris. She wanted to travel a little, too. How would she find time to look for the girls? She didn't know what they looked like, what their names were, or where they lived. Looking for them would be like trying to find a needle in a haystack. What was her father thinking? Natalie put the photos at the bottom of her suitcase. She did not intend to spend her semester in Paris looking for the little girls—grown women now—who had met her father thirty years ago.

When Natalie arrived in Paris, she immediately began making the most of her experience. During the week, she went to classes, and on long weekends she took train trips throughout Europe. The summer passed and the fall passed. The days got shorter, darker, and colder. Natalie was homesick. She missed her family. She missed her mother's cooking, and she missed hearing her parents speak Armenian. She remembered seeing a small stone Armenian church on a street in Paris. She decided to go there for a church service, just to hear Armenian spoken again.

When Natalie arrived at the church, she was surprised to see that it was crowded. She found a chair and sat down. A few minutes later, she saw a woman about 70 years old walking up and down the aisle on the other side of the church, looking for an empty chair. The woman was bent over and seemed to have trouble walking. Several people offered her their seats, but she shook her head, *no, no,* and kept walking in Natalie's direction. A few minutes later, she was standing next to Natalie.

Natalie stood up and, in Armenian, offered the woman her seat. The woman sat down. Natalie looked around; the only seat left was at the end of the row, against the stone wall, so Natalie sat down there. All through the service, the woman kept turning her head and staring at her. When the service ended, the woman asked her in Armenian, "You're not from here, are you?"

Natalie was dismayed. She had lived in the United States her whole life, but she had always spoken Armenian with her parents. She thought her Armenian was pretty good. She wondered if she spoke Armenian with an American accent.

"No, I'm not from here," Natalie answered. "How did you know?"

"I'm not from here, either," the woman answered. "I'm visiting my daughters. But I've noticed that the young Armenians, the ones who grow up here, don't speak Armenian. They all speak French. You speak Armenian—good Armenian—so I knew you weren't from here. Where are you from?"

"I'm from the United States, from Florida," Natalie answered.

"Ah, I have relatives in the United States," the woman said. She began to say their names: "Sarkis, Dikran, Ara…"

continued ▶

"Ara?" Natalie asked. Ara was Natalie's father's name. "When did you last see Ara?"

"Thirty years ago, in Syria," the woman answered. "He stayed with my family for a while on his way to the United States. Such a nice young man. He was so kind to my children."

Natalie began to cry. "That's my father," she said.

The woman began to cry, too, and raised her hands. "Asdoodzo Kordzeh," she said: God's work. "I've been looking for your father for thirty years. I knew you were something special. I knew it in your face."

Natalie had wanted to hear Armenian because she missed her family. She thought they were all thousands of miles away. Not all of them were far away. One of them was sitting near her, in a small stone church in Paris.

2 VOCABULARY

LOOKING AT THE STORY

Read each sentence. What is the meaning of the word(s) in *italics*? Write the letter of your answer on the line.

_j_ 1. Natalie was *packing* her suitcase.

_____ 2. Her father spoke to her in Armenian, his *native* language.

_____ 3. Natalie's father hoped that she would look for the girls *at some point* during her semester in Paris.

_____ 4. The children in the photos were *grown* women now.

_____ 5. Natalie thought that finding the girls would be *like looking for a needle in a haystack.*

_____ 6. Natalie didn't *intend* to look for the girls.

_____ 7. Natalie was *homesick*.

_____ 8. The woman in the church didn't stop when people asked her if she wanted to sit down. She *kept* walking toward Natalie.

_____ 9. Natalie stood up and *offered the woman her seat.*

_____ 10. The old woman *stared at her.*

_____ 11. Natalie thought her Armenian was pretty good, so she was *dismayed* when the woman said, "You're not from here, are you?"

_____ 12. As the woman *raised* her hands, she said, "Asdoodzo Kordzeh."

a. adult

b. almost impossible

c. asked the woman, "Would you like to sit here?"

d. continued

e. disappointed

f. first

g. lifted

h. looked at her for a long time

i. plan

j. putting clothes into

k. sad because she missed her home

l. sometime

LOOKING AT A NEW CONTEXT

A Answer the questions to show that you understand the meanings of the new words. You do not need to write complete sentences.

1. What are the languages of people who are born in your native country? _____
_____

2. Are you living in a new country? If so, name three things you packed in your suitcase (besides clothes) when you were getting ready to come. _____
_____

3. Do you have grown children? If so, write their names and ages. _____
_____

4. When guests come to your home, what do you offer them to eat and drink? _____
_____

5. What do you intend to do tomorrow? _____

6. What do you intend to do at some point? _____
_____

7. Name someone or something that would be so difficult to find, it would be like looking for a needle in a haystack. _____

B In small groups, take turns sharing your answers.

3 COMPREHENSION/READING SKILLS

UNDERSTANDING THE MAIN IDEAS

A Answer the questions. Write your answers on the lines. Write complete sentences.

1. Why was Natalie nervous and excited?
_____

2. How old was she?
_____

3. What did her father have in his hand?
_____

4. Who was the family in the photos?
_____

5. What was written on the back of the photos?
_____

B Write five questions of your own about the story. Then answer your questions. Begin your questions with one of these words:

Who   What   When   Where   Why   How

1. Q: _____

    A: _____

2. Q: _____

    A: _____

3. Q: _____

    A: _____

4. Q: _____

    A: _____

5. Q: _____

    A: _____

MAKING INFERENCES

Answer the questions. Write your answers on the lines. (The answers are not in the story, so you have to guess at the answers. Any logical guess is correct.)

1. Natalie was both excited and nervous about going to Paris. What do you think she was excited about? What do you think she was nervous about?

    _____

    _____

2. Why do you think Natalie sighed when she took the photos from her father?

    _____

    _____

3. Natalie made the most of her experience. During the week, she went to classes, and on long weekends she took train trips. What else do you think Natalie did to make the most of her time in France?

    _____

    _____

4. When Natalie arrived at the Armenian church, she was surprised to see that it was crowded. Why do you think she was surprised?

    _____

    _____

5. All through the service, the woman kept staring at Natalie. Why do you think she stared at her?

_____

_____

6. The story ends with Natalie meeting her father's cousin. What do you think happens next?

_____

_____

_____

4 DISCUSSION

Natalie's immediate family (her parents, brothers, and sisters) was in the United States. Her extended family (aunts, uncles, cousins, grandparents) was in Armenia, Syria, and France.

A Where is your immediate family? Put a star (✳) on those places on the map. Where is your extended family? Put an ✗ on those places on the map. Then show your map to a partner. Tell your partner about your family members and where they live.

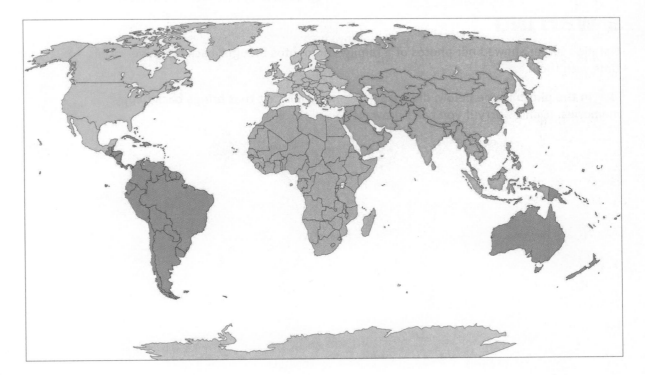

B Interview a partner about the languages your partner's family speaks. Write your partner's answers on the lines. (You do not need to write complete sentences.)

1. What languages does your family speak at home?

_____

2. Do you have children? If so, what language do they speak…

with you? _____

with one another? _____

at school? _____

with their friends? _____

3. Which language do you speak…

at work? _____

at school? _____

with your friends? _____

5 WRITING

Natalie's father showed her photos of a family. The photos brought back memories of his time with them.

A In the photo frame below, draw a scene from your past that brings back happy memories. (Don't worry if you can't draw well.)

B Write a paragraph about the scene. For example, one student drew a picture of herself and her father at the zoo and wrote this paragraph:

When I was a child, my father was very busy. So he rarely played with me. One Father's Day I drew a picture of his face. When I gave it to him, he smiled and said, "Thank you." That was all. But the next Sunday, he took me to the zoo. It was the first time we went out together. He stopped in front of the tigers for a long time, maybe 30 minutes. We were both born in the year of the Tiger. It was a silent and warm time. I remember it clearly.

_____

_____

_____

_____

_____

_____

_____

C Imagine this: You are looking at a photo of the people in your immediate family. On your own paper, write a paragraph about each person. Here is what one student wrote.

There are six people in my family. The members are Grandmother, Father, Mother, Elder Brother, Younger Brother, and I. We have almost the same faces, but we have different temperaments.

Grandmother is 66 years old. She is strong because she has done almost everything by herself. Her husband died in the war. Now she is retired, but sometimes she helps my parents. So she is still strong.

Father is a farmer. He cultivates flowers with Mother. I am just like him in looks and temperament.

Mother works on the farm and in the house. She works very hard.

Elder Brother is 25 and single. His job is fixing cars. He is quiet, but he has power because he is the oldest. So I follow him.

Younger Brother is 21 and single. He is active and very funny. His job is selling cars. The office of his company is far away from our house, so he lives alone.

Two university professors studied children like Natalie, who is the child of immigrants to the United States. Some of the children were born in the United States, and some came when they were small children. The professors begin their book *Legacies: The Story of the Immigrant Second Generation* by describing twelve immigrant children and their families. The following are three of the stories. The names of the children are fictitious, but the stories are true.

A **Read the stories.**

1 Alice

Alice lives with her parents, sister, and two brothers in a rented two-bedroom apartment. Her two brothers sleep in the living room, and Alice shares a bedroom with her sister. Although the apartment is small, it is tidy and has new furniture.

In their native country, Alice's mother worked for an insurance company and her father ran his own farm. But in the United States, her mother works as a waitress and her father delivers pizzas. They have both applied for green cards—which would make them permanent residents of the United States—but they have not received them yet.

Until they have their papers, they have to work at whatever jobs they can find.

Alice is fluent in English, forgetting her parents' language, and dreams of a brilliant American life. She gets excellent grades and is determined to go to college. Alice was not born in the United States, so she might not be eligible for college scholarships. Her parents don't know how they could possibly pay for a college education. Her mother says, "When children don't want to continue studying, that's one thing; you don't worry too much. But when you have a child who clearly has ambition, and you can't support her, it breaks your heart."

2 Jack

Jack came to the United States with his parents when he was eight years old. By the time he was 13, he felt totally American. He thought his parents were old-fashioned and authoritarian. They complained about his poor grades in school, talked about their own hard life, and told him he had to do better.

One day as Jack and his father were leaving the supermarket, his father asked him to carry the groceries to their old car and wait for him there while he ran another errand. "I'm not your slave," Jack replied. "Carry them yourself."

Jack's father responded as his own father would have in his native country: He slapped Jack twice on the side of his head and shook him by the shoulders. "Until you grow up, you'll do as you're told," he told his son.

Jack carried the groceries, but when he arrived at home, he called the police. His father was taken to the police station and charged with child abuse. Later, the father appeared before a judge who spoke the father's language. He did not send the father to jail but warned him that customs were different in the United States.

Jack's parents sent him back to their native country, where he is living with his grandparents and attending a private school. He cried and protested at first, but he is doing fine now.

His father says, "The U.S.A. is the strangest country in the world: the richest and most powerful, but twisted in knots as far as children are concerned. We had to send him back. We were losing him."

Kate

Kate is a 19-year-old university student. She came to the United States when she was seven years old. She and her eight brothers and sisters all do well in school. She says they were inspired by their older brother and tells this story:

"We were really not interested in school until my oldest brother graduated third in his high school class. That sort of opened our eyes. There was not much pressure to do very well until then, but once my brother did so well, that started us off…and everybody followed. The key thing is how the older ones start off, because if the older children start off on the wrong foot, it's very hard to get the younger ones on the right track. I have seen that happen, even to my relatives."

In Kate's family, the older brothers and sisters are responsible for helping the younger ones, so the entire family is a mini school system. Her second-oldest brother graduated from high school as class valedictorian, her third-oldest brother graduated fourth in his class, and Kate was class valedictorian. She says there is both cooperation and competition in her family. "We all urge one another to do better. It creates a good atmosphere. And helping my younger brothers and sisters gives me a good feeling."

Kate is a freshman at the University of California, majoring in chemistry. She says she hasn't done as well at the university as she had hoped, partly because there are a lot of students from her native country. She says they are very competitive, and they're almost all studying engineering, science, or math because they can't compete against Americans in English-based courses.

She says, "In my native country, you were taught at a much faster pace. I remember the things that I learned there in second grade were not taught in the United States until fourth or fifth grade. Math is the language we know, where we don't feel handicapped."

Kate wants to be a doctor.

B On your own paper, make a chart like this:

Sentences from the Stories	My Responses

C Choose three sentences from the stories that you would like to respond to. Copy the sentences word for word in the left column. In the right column, explain your response to each sentence. For example, you could begin your response:

The sentence surprised / confused me because…
The sentence made me feel happy / sad / angry because…
The sentence reminded me of my own experience because…
I agree / disagree with the opinion expressed in the sentence because…

UNIT 6

1 PRE-READING

Look at the picture and think about these questions. Discuss your answers with your classmates.

1. What do you see in the picture? What do you think happened?

2. The picture was taken at Pompeii. Where is Pompeii? Do you know what happened there?

The Buried City

Every year thousands of tourists visit Pompeii, Italy. They see the sights that Pompeii is famous for—its stadiums and theaters, its shops and restaurants. The tourists do not, however, see Pompeii's people. They do not see them because Pompeii has no people. No one has lived in Pompeii for almost 2,000 years.

Once Pompeii was a busy city of 22,000 people. It lay at the foot of Mount Vesuvius, a grass-covered volcano. Mount Vesuvius had not erupted for centuries, so the people of Pompeii felt safe. But they were not safe.

In August of the year 79, Mount Vesuvius erupted. The entire top of the mountain exploded, and a huge black cloud rose into the air. Soon, stones and hot ash began to fall on Pompeii. Then came a cloud of poisonous gas. When the eruption ended two days later, Pompeii was buried under 20 feet (6 meters) of stones and ash. Almost all of its people were dead.

Among the dead was a rich man named Diomedes. When the volcano erupted, Diomedes decided not to leave his home. The streets were filled with people who were running and screaming. Diomedes was probably afraid that he and his family would be crushed by the crowd. So Diomedes, his family, and their servants—sixteen people altogether—took some food and went down to the basement. For hours they waited in the dark, hoping the eruption would end. Then they began to cough. Poisonous gas from the mountain was filling the city. Diomedes realized that they had to leave. He took the key to the door, and a servant picked up a lantern. Together they walked upstairs. But the poisonous gas was already filling the house. When they were a few feet from the door, Diomedes and his servant fell to the floor and died. The other fourteen people downstairs died embracing one another.

For centuries, Diomedes and his family lay buried under stones and ash. Then, in the year 1861, an Italian archaeologist named Giuseppe Fiorelli began to uncover Pompeii. Slowly, carefully, Fiorelli and his men dug. The city they found looked almost the same as it had looked in the year 79. There were streets and fountains, houses and shops. There was a stadium with 20,000 seats. Perhaps most important of all, there were many everyday objects. These everyday objects tell us a great deal about the people who lived in Pompeii.

Many glasses and jars had a dark blue stain in the bottom, so we know that the people of Pompeii liked wine. They liked bread, too; metal bread pans were in every bakery. In one bakery oven, there were eighty-one round, flat loaves of bread—a type of bread that is still sold in Italy today. Tiny boxes filled with a dark, shiny powder tell us that the women liked to wear eye makeup, and the jewelry tells us that pearls were popular in the year 79. Graffiti was everywhere in Pompeii. On one wall, someone wrote, "Romula loves Staphyclus." On another wall, someone wrote, "Everyone writes on these walls—except me."

Fiorelli's discoveries tell us a lot about the way the people lived. They also tell us a lot about the way they died.

One day, Fiorelli was helping his men dig. When he tapped on the hard ash, he heard a hollow sound. He suspected that the space beneath was empty. As an experiment, he drilled a few holes in the ash and poured liquid plaster down the holes. When the plaster was hard, Fiorelli cleared away the ash. He found the plaster form of a man. The man's body had turned to dust long ago, but the ash had hardened around the space where the body had been.

During the following years, Fiorelli filled dozens of spaces with plaster. The plaster forms show how the people of Pompeii looked in their last moments of life. Some have calm expressions on their faces; others look very afraid. Some people died holding their children. Others died holding gold coins or jewelry. Diomedes died with a silver key in his right hand, and his servant died holding a lantern.

Giuseppe Fiorelli, too, has died, but his work continues. One-fourth of Pompeii has not been uncovered yet. Archaeologists are still digging, still making discoveries that draw the tourists to Pompeii.

2 VOCABULARY

LOOKING AT THE STORY

Read each sentence. What is the meaning of the word(s) in *italics*? Circle the letter of the correct answer.

1. Pompeii was *buried under* 20 feet of stones and ash.
   - (a.) covered by
   - b. hit by

2. Diomedes, his family, and their *servants* went down to the basement.
   - a. the people who worked in their home
   - b. the people who visited Pompeii

3. A servant picked up a *lantern*.
   - a. light
   - b. knife

4. The other fourteen people downstairs died *embracing one another*.
   - a. holding one another
   - b. arguing with one another

5. Slowly, carefully, Fiorelli and his men *dug*.

   a.
   b.

6. There were streets and *fountains*, houses and shops.

   a.
   b.

7. There was a *stadium* with 20,000 seats.
   - a. large indoor theater
   - b. large sports field with rows of seats around it

8. There were also everyday *objects* that tell us a great deal about the people who lived in Pompeii.
   - a. ideas
   - b. things

9. There were many glasses and jars with a dark blue *stain* in the bottom.
   - a. juice made from purple grapes
   - b. spot that can't be removed

10. *Graffiti* was everywhere in Pompeii.
    - a. writing on the walls
    - b. garbage

11. When he *tapped on* the hard ash, he heard a hollow sound.
    - a. hit lightly on
    - b. listened to

12. He *suspected that* the space beneath was empty.
    - a. told everyone that
    - b. thought that probably

LOOKING AT A NEW CONTEXT

A **Complete the sentences to show that you understand the meanings of the new words.**

1. Something often found buried under cities in my country is _____.

2. If I had servants, I would ask them to _____.

3. Someone I often embrace is _____.

4. An everyday object I have that tells a great deal about me is _____.

5. A good way to get a stain out of clothing is to _____.

6. If I were given permission to write graffiti on a city wall, I would write this: _____
_____.

7. Something that I suspect isn't true is _____.

B **In small groups, take turns reading your sentences aloud. Ask your classmates questions about their sentences.**

3 COMPREHENSION / READING SKILLS

UNDERSTANDING TIME RELATIONSHIPS

"The Buried City" describes Pompeii at three different times: around the year 79, in the 1860s, and today. Read the sentences from the story. Decide what time each sentence tells about. Put a check (✓) in the correct column.

	79	1860s	TODAY
1. Pompeii was a busy city of 22,000 people.	☑	☐	☐
2. Tourists see the sights Pompeii is famous for, but they do not see its people.	☐	☐	☐
3. Mount Vesuvius erupted.	☐	☐	☐
4. Giuseppe Fiorelli began to uncover the city.	☐	☐	☐
5. Jewelry made of pearls was popular.	☐	☐	☐
6. Diomedes, his family, and their servants died.	☐	☐	☐
7. Fiorelli poured liquid plaster down the holes in the ash.	☐	☐	☐
8. Someone wrote, "Romula loves Staphyclus," on a wall.	☐	☐	☐
9. Poisonous gas from the mountain filled the city.	☐	☐	☐
10. One-fourth of Pompeii is not yet uncovered.	☐	☐	☐

UNDERSTANDING CAUSE AND EFFECT

Find the best way to complete each sentence. Write the letter of your answer on the line.

1. Tourists do not see Pompeii's people __c__

2. The people of Pompeii felt safe _____

3. Diomedes decided not to leave his house _____

4. We know that the people of Pompeii liked bread _____

5. Fiorelli suspected that spaces beneath the ash were empty _____

a. because he was afraid that he and his family would be crushed by the crowd.

b. because he heard a hollow sound when he tapped on the ash.

c. because Pompeii has no people.

d. because Mount Vesuvius had not erupted for centuries.

e. because Fiorelli found metal bread pans in every bakery.

4 DISCUSSION

When the volcano erupted at Pompeii, people who left took their most important possessions.

A **Imagine this: Your home is on fire. Everyone who lives with you is safe, but your home will burn to the ground. There is time for you to save three of your possessions. Which possessions will you save?**

I will save...

1. _____

2. _____

3. _____

B **Why are the possessions on your list important? Are they expensive? Were they gifts from special people? Are they things you can't buy? Show your list to a partner. Explain why the things on your list are important to you.**

C **Draw a map of your native country. Then choose one of the following activities. In a small group, show your map to your classmates and discuss the answers to the questions.**

1. Are there any volcanoes in your country? Where are they? Mark them with a small mountain (∧) on your map. Do they erupt sometimes? Have you ever seen a volcanic eruption?

2. The people of Pompeii lived at the foot of a volcano. That was a dangerous place to live. Do people live in dangerous places in your country? Mark the places with an exclamation point (!) on your map. Why are those places dangerous? Why do people live there?

3. Are there places in your country that archaeologists have uncovered or are still uncovering? Mark the places with a star (✱) on your map.

5 WRITING

A On your own paper, write a description of one possession that is on the list you made in Exercise 4A. Explain why it is important to you. Here is what one student wrote.

> If I could save one possession, I would save the letters from my friends.
>
> Before I came to the United States, one of my friends wrote me this letter:
>
> "You will go to the United States soon. You may have many hard times before you adapt to your new environment. But don't forget that I am thinking of you all the time. Even if I'm not close to you, you'll always be in my heart."
>
> Every time I feel homesick, I read his letter. It always cheers me up. How could I ever replace a possession like that?

B Every year, thousands of tourists visit Pompeii. Have you ever been a tourist? Have you ever visited a beautiful or interesting place in your native country or in another country? Write about it on the lines below. Here is what one student wrote.

> ### My Visit to Kyoto, Japan
>
> I went to Kyoto in April this year. I stayed in a Japanese-style hotel. A mountain river ran past the hotel, and there was a wooden bridge over the river. From my hotel room, I could see a mountain. The mountain was many colors of green, and at the foot of the mountain, there were many cherry blossoms. The green colors and the cherry blossoms were reflected on the river. It was a beautiful view. My heart softened.

The following are five paragraphs that give more information about the people and places of Pompeii. On page 55, there are five photos.

A Read the paragraphs.

1

It appears that when Vesuvius erupted, less-wealthy people tried to leave the city, while wealthy Pompeiians stayed in their houses. The wealthy people were probably afraid that if they left, their houses would be looted when the eruption ended. So, they gathered up their most valuable possessions and ran to the strongest room in the house. When Fiorelli uncovered Pompeii, he sometimes found a whole family and their servants—all skeletons—together in one room of their house. The skeletons were surrounded by jewelry, coins, gold, and silver. In one house, a collection of beautiful silver was found hidden in the basement. All 115 pieces of silver were in perfect condition.

2

Houses in Pompeii did not have bathtubs because bathing was a recreational activity. Pompeii had four public baths, some for men and some for women. The layout of the baths indicates that bathers probably followed this routine: After checking their clothes, visitors took a cool bath to get clean. After the cool bath, they were massaged with fragrant oils. Then they were ready for the next four baths: a bath in warm water, a bath in very hot water (like the water in our Jacuzzis), another bath in warm water, and finally a bath in cool water. After their baths, the visitors could spend some time at the bath's library, swimming pool, or restaurant. Evidently, people stayed at the baths until well into the evening—1,300 lamps were found at one bath.

3

Visitors to Pompeii are amazed to see that some houses are identified by the owners' names. Signs in front of the houses say, for example, "This was the house of Diomedes" or "This was the house of Quintus Poppaeus." How did archaeologists learn the names of some Pompeiians and figure out exactly where they lived? Actually, it was quite simple. Many Pompeiians were businessmen who kept their business records on wax tablets. Their names were on the tablets. So, if wax tablets labeled "Diomedes" were found in a house, it is almost certain that Diomedes and his family lived there. In some cases, we know not only the names of the people who lived in a house, but also what those people looked like. In the house of a man named Jucundus, there was a bronze bust of a man—probably Jucundus himself. We know that Jucundus had big ears, thin hair, wrinkles on his forehead, and a large wart on his left cheek.

4

Pompeiians entertained themselves by watching gladiators fight. Pairs of gladiators, who were slaves or convicted criminals, generally fought until one man died. Gladiators who survived fight after brutal fight became heroes, much like our rock stars and great athletes. (When Pompeii was uncovered, the form of a woman wearing a lot of jewelry was found in the gladiators' barracks. Archaeologists speculate that she had gone there to catch a glimpse of her favorite hero.) The contests of the gladiators were so popular that Pompeiians built a stadium just for the fights. With 20,000 seats, the stadium held almost the entire population of Pompeii.

5

Imagine driving your car to a city—let's say, Paris—and discovering that you could not drive your car into Paris; you had to leave it parked outside the city. If you wanted to see Paris by car, you had to rent a Parisian car or travel by taxi. That was essentially the situation in Pompeii. Pompeii had a monopoly on transportation within its walls because of the way its streets were constructed. The stone streets of Pompeii filled with water during rainy weather. So that people could cross the streets without getting their feet wet, there were high blocks of stone at each intersection. The blocks of stone were always placed the same distance apart. Pompeiians knew what that distance was and built their chariots and carts so that the wheels passed on either side of the stepping stones. Few visitors to Pompeii had chariots that fit between the stepping stones, so most travelers had to leave their vehicles at the city gates. Cab drivers did a good business in Pompeii.

B Look at the photos. Which photo goes with which paragraph? Write the number of the paragraph on the line below the photo.

a. _____

b. _____

c. _____

d. _____

e. _____

PRE-READING

A Below are pairs of English words that sound alike. Your teacher will say one word from each pair. Circle the word that you hear.

1.	feel	fill	5.	cap	cup	9.	thick	sick	
2.	they	day	6.	glass	grass	10.	Jell-O	yellow	
3.	men	man	7.	hot	hat	11.	fifteen	fifty	
4.	ice	eyes	8.	thought	taught	12.	Oakland	Auckland	

B Your teacher will tell you which words she said and which words she didn't say. Which words were most difficult for you to hear the difference?

Misunderstandings

A woman from Australia was on vacation in California. On her first evening in California, she went to a restaurant for dinner.

"Are you ready to order?" the waiter asked her.

"Yes," she said. "I'll have the grilled salmon."

"Good choice," the waiter said. "The salmon came in fresh today. Your dinner comes with soup or salad."

"Sounds good," the woman said.

"The soup or salad?" the waiter asked.

"Yes," she said.

"You can only have one," the waiter said.

"That's fine," she said, sounding a little confused. "I only want one. It's big, right?"

"Which one?" the waiter asked.

"The salad," she replied.

"No, it's not really big," the waiter said. "If you want a big salad, there's a dinner salad on the menu. You can have grilled salmon on top of that."

"I'd rather have the salmon dinner," the woman said.

The waiter sighed. "OK," he said. "I'll bring you the salmon dinner. With salad."

"The super one, right?" the woman asked.

The waiter began to laugh, and a minute later the Australian woman was laughing, too. Now they both understood what was causing the confusion: The dinner came with either soup or salad—not a "super salad."

Similar-sounding English words also caused trouble for a man who wanted to fly from Los Angeles to Oakland, California—but this misunderstanding had more serious consequences. The man's problems began at the airport in Los Angeles. He thought he heard his flight announced, so he walked to the gate, showed his ticket, and got on the plane. Twenty minutes after takeoff, the man began to worry. Oakland was north of Los Angeles, but the plane seemed to be heading west, and when he looked out his window all he could see was ocean. "Is this plane going to Oakland?" he asked the flight attendant. The flight attendant gasped. "No," she said. "We're going to *Auckland*—Auckland, New Zealand."

Because so many English words sound similar, misunderstandings among English-speaking people are not uncommon. Every day, people speaking English ask one another questions like these: "Did you say seven*ty* or seven*teen*?" "Did you say that you *can* come or that you *can't*?" Similar-sounding words can be especially confusing for people whose native language is not English.

When a Korean woman who lives in the United States arrived at work one morning, her boss asked her, "Did you get a plate?" "No…," she answered, wondering what in the world he meant. She worked in an office. Why did the boss ask her about a plate? All day she wondered about her boss's strange question, but she was too embarrassed to ask him about it. At five o'clock, when she was getting ready to go home, her boss said, "Please be on time tomorrow. You were 15 minutes late this morning." "Sorry," she said. "My car wouldn't start, and…" Suddenly she stopped talking and began to smile. Now she understood. Her boss hadn't asked her, "Did you get a plate?" He had asked her, "Did you get up late?"

English is not the only language with similar-sounding words. Other languages, too, have words that can cause misunderstandings, especially for foreigners.

An English-speaking woman who was traveling in Mexico saw a sign in front of a restaurant. The sign said that the special that day was *"sopa con jamón y cebollas."* She knew that was Spanish for "soup with ham and onions." That sounded good. As the woman walked to her table, she practiced ordering. She whispered to herself, *"Sopa con jamón y cebollas. Sopa con jamón y cebollas."* Then she sat down, and a waiter came to take her order. *"Sopa con jabón y caballos,"* she said. "What?" the waiter asked. No wonder the waiter didn't understand. The woman had just ordered a very unusual lunch: soup with soap and horses.

"Soup or salad" and "super salad." *Auckland* and *Oakland*. "A plate" and "up late." *Jamón* and *jabón*. When similar-sounding words cause

continued ▶

a misunderstanding, probably the best thing to do is just laugh and learn from the mistake. Of course, sometimes it's hard to laugh. The man who traveled to Auckland instead of Oakland didn't feel like laughing. But even that misunderstanding turned out all right in the end. The airline paid for the man's hotel room and meals in New Zealand and for his flight back to California. "Oh well," the man later said, "I always wanted to see New Zealand."

2 VOCABULARY

LOOKING AT THE STORY

Read each sentence. What is the meaning of the word(s) in *italics*? Circle the letter of the correct answer.

1. The Australian woman thought the "super salad" *sounded good*.
   a. was a good idea
   b. had a musical sound

2. The waiter *sighed*. "OK," he said. "I'll bring you the salmon dinner. With salad."
   a. took in and let out a long, loud breath
   b. cried silently

3. Similar-sounding English words also caused trouble for a man who wanted to fly from Los Angeles to Oakland, California—but this misunderstanding *had more serious consequences*.
   a. made him laugh, although the situation was serious
   b. caused something more serious to happen

4. Twenty minutes after *takeoff*, the man began to worry.
   a. the plane went up into the air
   b. the man took off his jacket

5. "Is this plane going to Oakland?" he asked the *flight attendant*.
   a. person who flies an airplane
   b. person who takes care of the passengers on an airplane

6. Misunderstandings among English-speaking people are *not uncommon*.
   a. never happen
   b. happen often

7. Similar-sounding words can be especially confusing for people *whose native language is not English*.
   a. who do not like to speak English
   b. who didn't grow up speaking English

8. She *whispered* to herself, "Sopa con jamón y cebollas."
   a. talked very quietly
   b. thought very seriously

9. But even that misunderstanding *turned out all right in the end*.
   a. was OK after the plane turned back
   b. had a happy ending

LOOKING AT SPECIAL EXPRESSIONS

Find the best way to complete each sentence. Write the letter of your answer on the line.

I'd rather = **I prefer**

1. The Australian woman said, "I'd rather __b__

2. We could go to a theater, but I'd rather _____

3. There are two afternoon flights, but I'd rather _____

a. stay home and watch a movie on TV.

b. have the salmon dinner.

c. fly early in the morning.

in the world: This expression is used after a question word to show surprise.

4. "No, I didn't get a plate," she answered, wondering _____

5. When the phone rang at 1 a.m., he wondered _____

6. When we told her we were going for a walk, she asked us _____

d. why in the world we were going outside in such bad weather.

e. who in the world would call at that hour.

f. what in the world he meant.

no wonder = **it's not surprising**

7. No wonder the waiter didn't understand; _____

8. No wonder you're tired; _____

9. No wonder you didn't do well on the test; _____

g. you didn't go to bed until after midnight last night.

h. the woman had just ordered a very unusual lunch.

i. you didn't study.

to feel like = **to want to**

10. The man who traveled to Auckland instead of Oakland _____

11. Let's go to the party; _____

12. I'll eat just a sandwich; _____

j. I feel like dancing.

k. didn't feel like laughing.

l. I don't feel like eating a big dinner.

3 COMPREHENSION / READING SKILLS

UNDERSTANDING CAUSE AND EFFECT

Find the best way to complete each sentence. Write the letter of your answer on the line.

1. Misunderstandings among English-speakers are not uncommon __c__

2. The woman and the waiter had a misunderstanding _____

3. The man who wanted to fly to Oakland was worried _____

4. The Korean woman didn't ask her boss about his strange question _____

5. Her boss asked her, "Did you get up late?" _____

a. because she had arrived 15 minutes late.

b. because she heard "super salad," not "soup or salad."

c. because many English words sound similar.

d. because the plane seemed to be heading west, not north.

e. because she was too embarrassed.

UNDERSTANDING DETAILS

A Read the sentences from the story. One word in each sentence is *not* correct. Find the word and cross it out. Write the correct word.

1. Similar-sounding English words caused trouble for a man who wanted to fly from
   Los Angeles
   ~~Chicago~~ to Oakland, California.

2. Five minutes after takeoff, the man began to worry.

3. Oakland was south of Los Angeles.

4. When the man looked out his window, all he could see was desert.

5. The flight attendant smiled and said, "We're going to Auckland, New Zealand."

B Copy three other sentences from the story, but change one word in each sentence so that the information is *not* correct.

6. _____
   _____

7. _____
   _____

8. _____
   _____

C Give your sentences to a classmate. Your classmate will find the incorrect word in each sentence, cross it out, and write the correct word. When your classmate is finished, check the corrections.

4 DISCUSSION

A In a small group, tell your classmates about a time when you confused two similar-sounding words in English.

B The group will choose one story to act out in front of the class (with the permission of the person who told the story). People in the group will volunteer to play roles. The person who told the story will not take a role. He or she will be the "director."

C In your native language, are there similar-sounding words (like *seventy* and *seventeen*) that people sometimes confuse? What are the words? Tell the class.

5 WRITING

A Write the story you told your classmates in Exercise 4A. Here is what one student wrote.

After my family and I moved to the United States, I registered my daughter for school. I didn't speak much English then, so a woman at the elementary school helped me fill out the forms. When we were finished, she asked, "What size teacher do you want?" I didn't say anything. I was confused. She said, "Don't worry, the teachers are free. Each child gets one on the first day of school. What size do you want?" I still didn't understand.

Later I found out her question wasn't, "What size teacher do you want?" It was, "What size T-shirt do you want?"

B Have you ever had a misunderstanding about food? Have you ever had a problem eating at someone's house, buying food at a supermarket, or ordering food at a restaurant? Write about your experience. Here is what one student wrote.

On a visit to the United States, I went to a restaurant with my friends. I ordered a salad. The waitress asked me, "What kind of dressing do you want on your salad—blue cheese, ranch, Italian, or French?" Of course, I said "French" because I am French. When the waitress brought the salad, I was shocked. The dressing was orange. I had never seen dressing like that in France. Then I tasted it. It tasted terrible. I never ordered "French" dressing again.

CHALLENGE

Some English words and phrases sound so alike that they confuse even native speakers—people who have been speaking English all their lives.

A Read about some mistakes that people in the United States—all native speakers—made. Which words did they confuse? Look at the words below. Write your answer on the line: Work with a partner.

answer	onion	self-esteem	X-rayed
fried egg	only	tennis shoes	Youth in Asia
ice cream	sauce	which it stands	

1

A little boy asked his mother to make him a "Friday sandwich." The boy didn't really want a "Friday" between two slices of bread. What did he want? He wanted a _____ sandwich.

2

A teacher asked a seven-year-old girl if she had any brothers or sisters. "No," the girl answered. "I'm a lonely child." Actually, the expression isn't "a lonely child"; it's "an _____ child."

3

A young woman went to a movie with her boyfriend. As they were driving home, her boyfriend turned to her and said, "I'm going to take you to a place where they have the best diamond rings in the world." The woman was excited. Her boyfriend was going to buy her a diamond ring! A few minutes later, her boyfriend pulled into the drive-thru of a fast-food restaurant. When he ordered the food, the woman realized that her boyfriend hadn't said "the best diamond rings." He had said "the best _____ rings."

4

A little girl went to a Mexican restaurant with her family. When the waitress put the little girl's dinner down in front of her, she covered her meal with her hands and told her parents, "Please don't put any hot socks on my food." Actually, it wasn't hot socks that she didn't like; it was hot _____.

5

A woman who hurt her arm went to the emergency room of a hospital. Doctors checked her arm and told her it was not badly hurt. After the woman left the hospital, a nurse wrote this on the woman's medical chart: "Patient was examined, X-rated, and sent home." Movies are sometimes X-rated, but patients are _____.

6

A teenaged girl wrote a letter to her girlfriend. She told her friend that her boyfriend had broken up with her, and now she didn't feel good about herself. She wrote that he hurt her "self of steam." Actually, the expression "self of steam" doesn't exist in English. She meant to say that the boy had hurt her _____.

A teacher asked her students to name famous Americans in history. One boy replied, "Richard Stans." The teacher was puzzled. She had never heard of Richard Stans. "Who is he?" she asked the boy. "I'm not sure," the boy answered, "but he must be very important. Every morning we all stand and face the flag. Then we say, 'I pledge allegiance to the flag of the United States of America, and to the republic for Richard Stans.'" The teacher had to laugh. The boy had misunderstood the correct words, which are: "I pledge allegiance to the flag of the United States of America, and to the republic for _____."

A large department store had an optical department where people could get eye exams and buy glasses. One day the optical department was giving free eye exams. So, this was announced over the store's public address system: "The optical department is giving a free eye screening today." A lot of people who were shopping at the store heard the announcement and hurried to the optical department, where a long line formed. It turned out, however, that the people weren't waiting for a free eye screening; they were waiting for free _____.

9

High school students who took a public speaking class had to give a speech. One student chose as her topic euthanasia—the painless killing of people who are incurably sick. After she gave her speech, one student said to another, "Her speech was interesting. But she didn't say anything about teenagers in countries like Japan and China." The student thought the title of the speech was not "Euthanasia," but "_____."

10

A magazine advertised over the radio. The magazine offered a special price of $19.95 for a subscription. For $19.95, people would receive ten issues of the magazine. When some people called the magazine's toll-free number to place their orders, they gave their credit card numbers and then their shoe sizes. Why did they give their shoe sizes? The people had misunderstood the words *ten issues*. They thought they were ordering _____.

11

A teenaged boy was listening to the Bob Dylan song "Blowin' in the Wind" for the first time. "I think it's a great song," he told his father. "But I don't understand the line about the ants. Why is he singing, 'The ants are my friends, blowin' in the wind'?" Actually, that is not what Bob Dylan sings. He sings, "The _____, my friend, is blowin' in the wind."

B Report your answers back to the class.

C Ask your teacher to read each mistake and then the correct answer. Can you hear any differences in pronunciation?

Ed Jones (on the right) and the map

1 PRE-READING

**Look at the picture and think about these questions. Discuss your answers with
your classmates.**

1. What is a thrift store?

2. Have you ever been to a thrift store? What things were for sale there? Tell your teacher.
   Your teacher will make a list on the board.

3. In your native country, do you have thrift stores or other places where you can buy things
   cheaply? Describe them to your classmates.

4. The men in the picture are looking at something that one of the men bought at a thrift
   store. What do you think it is? Why do you think the man on the right looks happy?

A Real Bargain

In his spare time, Ed Jones likes to shop at thrift stores. He looks for things that might be valuable—old dishes or used books, for example. If he finds something valuable, he buys it cheaply and then resells it to an antique dealer.

One day Mr. Jones was shopping at a thrift store in Indianapolis, Indiana, and not having much luck. He didn't see anything he wanted, so he started walking toward the door. Then something caught his eye. Leaning against a wall, there was a large cardboard map. He walked over for a closer look.

The map was covered with dust, so Mr. Jones wiped it with his handkerchief. Under the dust was a color map of Paris. It looked old. On the back of the map, someone had written the price: $3. Mr. Jones was quite certain that the map was worth more than $3, so he bought it. He thought he could probably sell it for $40.

Later, at home, Mr. Jones looked more closely at the map. He decided it might be very old. Maybe it was worth even more than $40.

The next day, Mr. Jones took the map to a geography professor at a nearby university. The professor was a map expert. After looking at the map for a few minutes, he became very excited. "I've read about this map!" he exclaimed. Then he told Mr. Jones what he knew.

In 1671, the king of France, Louis XIV, asked a cartographer to make a map of Paris. The cartographer worked on the map for four years. The map he drew was beautiful—it was not just a map, but a work of art as well. The cartographer made several black-and-white copies of the map. Then he carefully colored one of the copies, using blue for rivers, green for trees, and brown for buildings. The professor said that one black-and-white copy of the map was in the British Museum in London, and another was in the Bibliothèque Nationale in Paris. "I think," the professor told Mr. Jones, "that you've just found the color copy of the map—in a thrift store in Indianapolis!" The professor suggested that Mr. Jones take the map to New York City. Experts there could tell Mr. Jones if the professor was right.

The New York experts said the professor was right. They told Mr. Jones that he had the only color copy of the map and that it was extremely valuable. "How much do you think it's worth?" Mr. Jones asked the experts. "Millions," they replied. "It's impossible to say exactly how much the map is worth. It's worth whatever someone is willing to pay for it."

Soon Mr. Jones discovered how much people were willing to pay for the map. Someone offered him $10 million; then someone else immediately offered him $12 million. The next offer was $19.5 million. Of course, those were only offers—not money. But the offers told Mr. Jones that the experts were right—the map was extremely valuable.

How in the world did this map find its way to a thrift store in Indianapolis? Here is what some experts think: The map was probably in a museum or in the home of a wealthy family in France. Then, a thief stole it, perhaps during the confusion of World War I or World War II. The thief sold the map to an antique dealer in France. The French antique dealer, not knowing how valuable the map was, sold it to an antique dealer in Indianapolis. That antique dealer, who also did not know its value, gave it to a neighbor. For ten years, the map hung on a wall in the neighbor's house. Then the neighbor got tired of it and sold it to the thrift store. The map sat in the thrift store for months. Finally Mr. Jones discovered it.

When Mr. Jones went shopping at the thrift store, he was looking for a bargain. He wanted to find something that was worth more than the price he paid. He paid $3 for the map, and it is probably worth millions. Now, that's a bargain!

2 VOCABULARY

LOOKING AT THE STORY

Read each sentence. What is the meaning of the word(s) in *italics*? Circle the letter of the correct answer.

1. Ed Jones was shopping at a *thrift store*.
   - **a.** store that sells used things at low prices
   - **b.** store that sells expensive things at high prices

2. If he found something valuable, he could resell it, perhaps to an *antique dealer*.
   - **a.** person who fixes broken things
   - **b.** person who buys and sells old things

3. Leaning against a wall of the store, there was a large *cardboard* map.
   - **a.** made of heavy paper
   - **b.** made of plastic

4. Mr. Jones was quite *certain* that the map was worth more than $3.
   - **a.** worried
   - **b.** sure

5. The next day, Mr. Jones took the map to a *geography* professor at a nearby university.
   - **a.** the study of the world's countries, cities, oceans, rivers, and mountains
   - **b.** the study of the world's history, languages, and customs

6. The professor was a map *expert*.
   - **a.** person who draws maps
   - **b.** person with special knowledge

7. "I've read about this map!" he *exclaimed*.
   - **a.** said with strong feeling
   - **b.** said very quietly

8. Louis XIV asked a *cartographer* to make a map of Paris.
   - **a.** person who draws maps
   - **b.** person who writes books

9. The New York experts told Mr. Jones that his map was *extremely* valuable.
   - **a.** not really
   - **b.** very

10. "How much do you think it's worth?" Mr. Jones asked the experts. "Millions," they *replied*.
    - **a.** answered
    - **b.** asked

11. Someone *offered him $10 million*.
    - **a.** said, "Will you take $10 million for the map?"
    - **b.** told him, "I think your map is worth $10 million."

12. Some experts think the map was probably in a museum or in the home of a *wealthy* family in France.
    - **a.** famous
    - **b.** rich

13. When Mr. Jones went shopping at the thrift store, he was looking for a *bargain*.
    - **a.** something that can be bought cheaply
    - **b.** something that has been used

LOOKING AT SPECIAL EXPRESSIONS

Find the best way to complete each sentence. Write the letter of your answer on the line.

to catch someone's eye = **to get someone's attention**

1. Mr. Jones was walking toward the door ___b___

2. She was leaving the museum _____

3. He was walking through the department store _____

   a. when a painting by Renoir caught her eye.

   b. when a large cardboard map caught his eye.

   c. when a sweater caught his eye.

to be worth = **to have a value of**

4. Mr. Jones was quite certain that _____

5. They paid $80,000 for their house, but _____

6. He tried to sell his old TV for $500, but nobody bought it because _____

   d. the map was worth more than $3.

   e. it wasn't worth more than $250.

   f. it was worth at least $100,000.

to be willing to = **to be ready to**

7. The map was worth whatever _____

8. Our teacher said that _____

9. I won't have to take the bus home because _____

   g. he was willing to give us extra help after class.

   h. my friend is willing to give me a ride.

   i. someone was willing to pay for it.

to get tired of = **to become no longer interested in**

10. The neighbor got tired of the map and _____

11. He got tired of hamburgers _____

12. I'm getting tired of studying French; _____

   j. after eating them every day for a month.

   k. sold it to a thrift store.

   l. maybe I'll study Spanish next year.

3 COMPREHENSION / READING SKILLS

UNDERSTANDING CAUSE AND EFFECT

Find the best way to complete each sentence. Write the letter of your answer on the line.

1. Ed Jones went to the thrift store ___c___

2. He wiped the map with his handkerchief _____

3. The professor suggested that Mr. Jones take the map to New York City _____

4. Experts in New York said the map was extremely valuable _____

5. The map was a bargain _____

   a. because experts there could tell Mr. Jones if the professor was right.

   b. because it was cheap but very valuable.

   c. because he was looking for a bargain.

   d. because it was the only color copy.

   e. because it was covered with dust.

UNDERSTANDING DETAILS

A Read the sentences from the story. One word in each sentence is *not* correct. Find the word and cross it out. Write the correct word.

1. The map was covered with ~~paint~~. *dust*

2. Under the dust was a color map of Rome.

3. The map looked new.

4. On the back of the map, someone had written the price: $30.

5. The next day, Mr. Jones took the map to a mathematics professor at a nearby university.

B Copy three other sentences from the story, but change one word in each sentence so that the information is *not* correct.

6. _____

_____

7. _____

_____

8. _____

_____

C Give your sentences to a partner. Your partner will find the incorrect word in each sentence, cross it out, and write the correct word. When your partner is finished, check the corrections.

4 DISCUSSION

Mr. Jones bought a map at a low price and then discovered it was worth a lot more than he paid for it.

A Tell your classmates about one of the following experiences.

- You bought something at a low price and then discovered it was worth more than you paid for it.

- You bought something at a high price and then discovered that it was worth less than you paid for it.

B What would you do if you suddenly had millions of dollars? How would you use the money? Make a list of what you would do.

1. _____

2. _____

3. _____

4. _____

5. _____

C Read your list to a partner. Tell your partner what you would do and why.

5 WRITING

The word *bargain* is both a noun and a verb. *A bargain* is something that is bought at a cheap price, like Mr. Jones's map. *To bargain* is to talk in order to get a good price.

A Imagine this: You are at an open-air market. You see something you want to buy and you ask about the price. It is too high, so you start to walk away. The seller starts to bargain with you. What does the seller say? What do you say? Write a conversation between you and the seller. Each person should speak six to eight times.

B Write a story. It could be a true story (for example, the one that you told your classmates in Exercise 4A), or it could be a story that you imagine. In the story, describe something you bought cheaply and later discovered was very valuable. This is what one student wrote.

I bought a dress at a thrift store. It was red and made of lace. It was only $1.

I wore the dress to a party. A woman at the party stared at me for a long time. Then she asked me, "Where did you get that dress?" "I got it from a friend," I answered. That was not true, but I didn't want to say that I had bought it at a thrift store for only $1. "That was Miss K's dress," the woman said. "She wore it at her last concert." (Miss K was a famous singer.) "I'm a great fan of Miss K's," the woman continued. "I have all her CDs, and I have many photographs of her. But I don't have anything that she wore. Will you please sell me that dress? I don't know what your friend paid for it, but I'm willing to pay $500."

I told her she could have the dress for $500 and went home from the party very happy.

Ed Jones's $3 map is probably worth millions of dollars. Can you guess what the items below are worth? All of these valuable items were sold at auctions. The most valuable item sold for $11.7 million. The least valuable item sold for $38,000.

A Read the descriptions of the items.

1 Letter Handwritten by Abraham Lincoln

Abraham Lincoln was president of the United States during the Civil War (1861–1865), when the Southern states fought the Northern states over the issue of slavery. The Southern states wanted to separate from the United States.

When the Civil War began, a man named William McCullough wanted to fight for the North. The army rejected him because he was blind in one eye. McCullough had once worked for Lincoln, and he asked the president for help. President Lincoln intervened, and the army accepted McCullough. He was killed in battle.

McCullough's daughter, Fanny, was distraught over her father's death, and Lincoln wrote her a letter of condolence. He began his letter, "It is with deep grief that I learn of the death of your kind and brave father." Then he offered Fanny some comforting words: "You cannot now realize that you will ever feel better. Is this not so? And yet it is a mistake. You are sure to be happy again. To know this, which is certainly true, will make your sorrow less miserable now.

I have had experience enough to know what I say; and you need only to believe it, to feel better now."

Lincoln's letter to Fanny is considered to be one of the greatest condolence letters ever written.

2 Andy Warhol Soup-Can Painting

The painter Andy Warhol was one of the most influential artists of the twentieth century. His style of painting is called Pop Art because he took popular, common images and transformed them into art. He is perhaps most famous for his soup-can paintings, which he completed in 1961 and 1962. There are thirty-two paintings of soup cans, and each painting is slightly different. When the paintings first went on sale, they sold for $100 each. Now a Warhol soup-can painting sells for many times that amount.

Andy Warhol died in New York City in 1987. On the 20th anniversary of his death, the National

Gallery of Scotland wrapped the columns of its museum with pictures of soup cans in his honor.

3 Steiff Teddy Bear

Margarete Steiff, a German woman, created the first teddy bear more than 100 years ago. Ms. Steiff wasn't originally a toy maker; she was a seamstress who fell into toy-making by chance.

Margarete had polio as an infant, and she was never able to walk. So, when she became a young woman, she needed to find work she could do while sitting in a wheelchair. She decided to become a seamstress. By the time she was 25, Margarete was earning a good living making dresses for wealthy women.

One day Margarete was looking through a fashion magazine and spotted a pattern for a toy elephant made of cloth. She made several elephants and gave them to friends as gifts. Her friends loved their toy elephants and encouraged Margarete to make more cloth toys. She began making little bears, dogs, and donkeys, and selling them, in addition to selling dresses.

By 1897, Margarete was selling more toys than dresses; in fact, she was selling so many toys, she had to hire forty women to help her sew them. The most popular toys were the cloth bears.

Margarete's nephew took some of the "Steiff bears" to the United States, where they became an instant hit. In the United States, the bears were called "teddy bears," named after President Theodore Roosevelt, whose nickname was Teddy.

The Steiff Company is still in business in Germany. New Steiff teddy bears, like the one in the photo, are quite expensive because they are made by hand. It is the old teddy bears, however–the ones that Margaret Steiff and her 40 employees made–that are really valuable. A 1905 Steiff bear, in almost perfect condition, sold for considerably more than the bear in the photo.

4 Diana's Velvet Dress

In 1997, Diana, Princess of Wales, decided to auction off some of her evening dresses and to give the money to charity. The auction took place in New York City in June, two months before her death. On the evening of the auction, the auction house was packed with people, and fifty telephone lines connected the auction to bidders all over the world.

That evening, this velvet evening gown brought the highest price. Princess Diana had worn the dress to a dinner at the White House with U.S. president Ronald Reagan and his wife, Nancy. Princess Diana was a fan of Hollywood movies, so the Reagans invited several movie stars to the dinner. After dinner, Diana danced with one of her favorite actors, John Travolta. The next morning, newspapers all over the world carried photos of Diana dancing in her velvet gown.

B Take a guess: Which item do you think sold for $11.7 million? Which one do you think sold for $38,000? Then check the Key on page 138 to see how much these items sold for.

UNIT 9

1 PRE-READING

A Are you superstitious? Read the statements. Then check (✓) *YES* or *NO*.

		YES	NO
1.	Black cats are unlucky.	☐	☐
2.	It is unlucky to break a mirror.	☐	☐
3.	If I point at the moon, something bad will happen to me.	☐	☐
4.	It is bad luck when a shoelace breaks.	☐	☐
5.	If my palm itches, I will receive money.	☐	☐
6.	When I want good luck, I sometimes cross my fingers or knock on wood.	☐	☐
7.	I have a lucky number.	☐	☐
8.	I have something that I consider lucky—a lucky pen or a lucky hat, for example.	☐	☐

B If you checked *Yes* after any of these statements, you are probably a little superstitious. What about your classmates? Are they superstitious? Discuss the following questions.

1. Who in your class is superstitious?

2. Who in your class is not superstitious?

Black Cats and Broken Mirrors

Do you think that it is bad luck to walk under a ladder or break a mirror? Do you think that black cats and the number 13 are unlucky? Do you have a lucky number? Do you have a lucky shirt, hat, or pen? If you answered "yes" to any of those questions, you might be superstitious. But don't worry—you're not alone. There are more than one million superstitions, and most people believe at least one or two of them.

Many people are superstitious about numbers. They think that there are lucky numbers and unlucky numbers. The number 13 is often considered unlucky. In some parts of the world, buildings have no thirteenth floor and streets have no houses with the number 13. In Japan, the number 4 is considered unlucky because in Japanese, the word *four* is pronounced the same as the word *death*. Japanese never give gifts of four knives, four napkins, or four of anything.

What are lucky numbers? Seven is a lucky number in many places, and the number 8 is considered lucky in Japan and China. In China, businesses often open on August 8 (8/8), and many couples register to get married at eight minutes past eight o'clock on August 8.

Superstitions about numbers are so widespread that some people—called numerologists—make a living giving advice about numbers. In 1937, when the Toyoda family of Japan wanted to form a car company, they asked a numerologist if "Toyoda" would be a good name for the company. The numerologist said it would not be. He explained that "Toyoda" took ten strokes of the pen to write, and 10 was not a lucky number. "Toyota," however, took eight strokes to write, and 8 was a very lucky number. The numerologist recommended "Toyota" as a better name for the company. The family took his advice. As a result, millions of people drive "Toyotas" and not "Toyodas."

In addition to superstitions about numbers, there are many other kinds of superstitions. There are superstitions about eating, sleeping, sneezing, and itching. There are superstitions about animals and holidays and horseshoes. There are even superstitions about superstitions.

Those superstitions tell people how to reverse bad luck.

For example, in many parts of the world, spilling salt is bad luck. Throwing salt, however, is good luck. So, people who spill salt throw a little of the spilled salt over their left shoulder. Throwing the spilled salt reverses the bad luck. When the Japanese bump heads, they immediately bump heads again. According to a Japanese superstition, the first bump means their parents will die, but the second bump "erases" the first bump. To reverse bad luck in general, people turn around three times, turn their pockets inside out, or put their hats on backwards. In the United States, baseball players sometimes wear their caps inside out and backwards when their team is losing. It looks silly, but the baseball players don't mind if it helps them win the game.

Because there are so many superstitions, it is not surprising that some of them are contradictory. In Germany, it is good luck when the left eye twitches and bad luck when the right eye twitches. In Malaysia, it is exactly the opposite: A twitching right eye means good luck, and a twitching left eye means bad luck. Accidentally putting on clothes inside out brings good luck in Pakistan but bad luck in Costa Rica. In Chile, unmarried people won't take the last piece of food on the plate because it means they will never marry. In Thailand, unmarried people take the last piece because it means they will marry someone good-looking.

Some superstitions have been with us for so long that they have become customs. In many parts of the world, it is polite to say "Health" or "God bless you" when someone sneezes. People used to think that the soul could escape from the body during a sneeze. They said "God bless you" to protect people from losing their souls. Today, we no longer believe that people who sneeze are in danger of losing their souls, but we say "God bless you" anyway. We say it not because we are superstitious, but because we are polite.

Almost everyone is at least a little superstitious—even people who say they aren't.

continued ▶

One woman says that when she got married, her aunt gave her white bath towels. "Never buy purple towels," her aunt said. "If you use purple towels, your marriage will end." Does the woman believe that superstition? "No, of course not," she says. "It's silly." Does she use purple towels? "Well, no," she answers. "Why take chances?

2 VOCABULARY

LOOKING AT THE STORY

Read each sentence. What is (or shows) the meaning of the word(s) in *italics*? Circle the letter of the correct answer.

1. Do you think that it is bad luck to walk under a *ladder*?

   a.   b.

2. If you answered "yes" to any of those questions, *you might be* superstitious.

   a. you are definitely   b. maybe you are

3. Superstitions about numbers are *widespread*.

   a. found in many places   b. believed only by children

4. Some people *make a living* giving people advice about numbers.

   a. make money   b. make mistakes

5. "Toyota" took *eight strokes* of the pen to write.

   a. 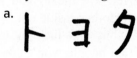   b.

6. The family *took his advice*.

   a. did what he suggested   b. asked for more information

7. There are superstitions that *reverse bad luck*.

   a. change bad luck to good luck   b. give the bad luck to someone else

8. If you *spill salt*, immediately throw a little of the spilled salt over your left shoulder.

   a. use too much salt   b. pour out salt accidentally

9. It looks silly, but the baseball players *don't mind* if it helps them win the game.

   a. think that's OK   b. don't like to think about it

10. Some superstitions *are contradictory*. In Germany, it is good luck when the left eye twitches. In Malaysia, it is bad luck when the left eye twitches.

    a. are very old   b. mean the opposite

11. Accidentally putting clothes on *inside out* brings good luck in Pakistan.

    a. in the house, rather than outside   b. with the inside parts on the outside

12. People used to think that the soul could *escape from* the body during a sneeze.

    a. enter   b. leave

LOOKING AT SPECIAL EXPRESSIONS

Find the best way to complete each sentence. Write the letter of your answer on the line.

as a result = **because of that**

1. The family took the numerologist's advice.
   As a result, ___c___

2. He overslept. As a result, _____

3. She didn't study. As a result, _____

a. he was late for work.

b. she didn't do well on the test.

c. millions of people today drive "Toyotas" and not "Toyodas."

in addition to = **as well as** ("In addition to" connects two similar ideas.)

4. In addition to the superstitions about numbers, _____

5. In addition to studying French, _____

6. In addition to being an excellent student, _____

d. she's an excellent dancer and swimmer.

e. there are many other kinds of superstitions.

f. he's studying German and Spanish.

according to X = **X says / shows that**

7. According to a Japanese superstition, _____

8. According to my watch, _____

9. According to this map, _____

g. the museum is on Michigan Avenue.

h. the first bumping of heads means your parents will die.

i. it's a quarter to nine.

3 COMPREHENSION / READING SKILLS

UNDERSTANDING THE MAIN IDEAS

What information is not in the story? Cross out the three sentences with information that is *not* in the story.

1. There are over one million superstitions.

2. Children are usually not superstitious.

3. Many people are superstitious about numbers.

4. Numerologists make a living giving people advice about numbers.

5. It is always a good idea to take a numerologist's advice.

6. Some superstitions tell people how to reverse bad luck.

7. Some superstitions are contradictory.

8. Some superstitions have become customs.

9. People who use purple towels are silly.

10. Almost everyone is at least a little superstitious.

UNDERSTANDING SUPPORTING DETAILS

Find the best way to complete each sentence. Write the letter of your answer on the line.

1. Many people are superstitious about numbers. For example, _c_

2. Some people—called numerologists—make a living giving people advice about numbers. For example, _____

3. There are superstitions that tell people how to reverse bad luck. For example, _____

4. Some superstitions are contradictory. For example, _____

5. Some superstitions have been with us for so long that they have become customs. For example, _____

a. accidentally putting on clothes inside out brings good luck in Pakistan but bad luck in Costa Rica.

b. it is polite to say "Health" or "God bless you" when someone sneezes.

c. the number 13 is often considered unlucky.

d. throwing spilled salt over the left shoulder reverses bad luck.

e. a numerologist recommended "Toyota" as the name for the car company.

4 DISCUSSION

Form small conversation groups. Ask the people in your group if they know any superstitions about the following.

salt	garlic	cooking
ladders	four-leaf clovers	eating a pear
mirrors	numbers	dropping silverware
brooms	hiccups	chopsticks
combs	itching	sleeping
knives	sneezing	dreams
shoes	ears ringing	leaving the house
black cats	eye twitching	finding a coin
crows	shivering	opening an umbrella
owls	whistling	knocking on wood
rabbits	cutting nails	weddings
elephants	taking photos	New Year's Day
horseshoes	giving gifts	funeral processions

5 WRITING

A Make a list of superstitions that some people in your native country believe. Here is an example from a student from Panama.

1. Always sleep with your feet facing the door of your room.
2. If you give your sweetheart a handkerchief or socks, you will argue.
3. If you want a visitor to leave, turn your broom upside down.
4. If a young woman is sweeping the floor and the broom accidentally touches her feet, she will marry a rich old man.
5. To protect yourself from evil spirits, wear your pajamas inside out.

B Write about something you have that is lucky—a lucky number or a lucky hat, for example. Why is it lucky? Can you remember a time when it brought you good luck? Here is what one student wrote.

When I was a high school student, I had a difficult mathematics test one day. Before the test, our teacher told us, "Use the same pencil you used when you studied last night. When you can't solve a problem, hold the pencil tightly. If you do that, you will be able to solve the problem." I did that, and I got every answer right. I thought, "This is my lucky pencil." But later I discovered that my pencil was lucky only sometimes. When I studied hard, my pencil helped me, but when I didn't study hard, it didn't help me.

C Has there ever been a time when you've had very good—or very bad—luck? Write about it. Here is what one student wrote.

Last month, I had a very unlucky day. I overslept in the morning because I had forgotten to set my alarm clock. It was raining. On the way to the bus stop, I fell and got wet. Then I missed the bus and was late for my class.

That night a friend of mine called me while I was cooking dinner. It was a long phone call, and I forgot about my dinner. When I finished talking to my friend, I went into the kitchen to check on my dinner. It was burned. I thought, "I have only two hands and one head. I'm trying to do too much." But later I thought, "I was just not lucky today."

CHALLENGE

Many superstitions and customs that are common in the United States are actually thousands of years old. They have their origins in ancient beliefs.

A Read about these ancient beliefs.

1

The ancient Greeks had many gods and goddesses. The goddess of the moon, marriage, and childbirth was Artemis. On Artemis's birthday, people baked moon-shaped cakes and brought them to her temple. They also brought candles to the temple and placed them on the altars there. All the candles were lit and then blown out at the same time. If the people blew out all the candles in one communal breath, Artemis was happy with her worshipers. If some candles remained lit, Artemis was unhappy.

2

In ancient Asia, people who were sentenced to death were hanged. Sometimes they were hanged from trees, and sometimes they were hanged from the seventh rung of a ladder that was placed against a building. People believed that the space under a ladder that had been used for a hanging was dangerous because the spirit of the dead person could linger there long after the body was gone.

3

Between the Middle Ages and the eighteenth century, witch hunts were common in Europe. People believed they had to find witches and kill them, as witches had the power to do great harm. The suspected "witches" were typically old women who were eccentric and who lived alone. Old women who had cats were especially feared because people believed that cats could be demons who had taken the shape of a cat. The fear of witches eventually subsided, but fear of cats—particularly black cats—remained.

4

Long ago, the people who lived in present-day Europe believed that gods lived in trees. Perhaps they came to this conclusion because lightning often strikes trees. Or perhaps they saw trees losing their leaves in the autumn and growing new leaves in the spring and thought that gods and goddesses inside the trees were making these seasonal changes. At any rate, ancient people believed that trees (especially oak trees) had divine power. When people had a favor to ask, they knocked on a tree to let the resident god know they were there and then made their request. If the request was granted, they returned to the tree and knocked a few times to say "thank you."

5

An ancient legend goes something like this: A king with three daughters asks each one to describe how much she loves him. The oldest daughter says she loves him as much as bread. The middle daughter says she loves him as much as wine. The youngest daughter says she loves him as much as salt. The king is furious that his youngest daughter compared her love for him with her love for salt, and he says she must leave the palace. She leaves, but secretly she meets with the palace cook. She asks the cook to leave salt out of her father's meals. The king realizes the importance of salt and calls his youngest daughter back. This story was told by the Romans 2,000 years ago. Salt was important not only to them, but also to people throughout the ancient world. It was used to preserve and flavor food, and it was so valuable that it was considered almost supernatural.

Two thousand years ago, the Etruscans—people who lived in what is now central Italy—used chickens to tell the future. The Etruscans would draw a circle on the ground, divide the circle into sections—one section for each letter of the alphabet—and put kernels of corn in each section. Then they put a chicken in the circle and observed the chicken as it picked up corn. For example, if a young woman wanted to know the first letter of her future husband's name, she would ask that question and then watch to see which section of the circle the chicken went to. After the chicken did its work, it was killed and its collarbone was hung out to dry. Two people then made a wish on the bone. One person held on to one end of the bone while another person held on to the other end. Then both people pulled. When the bone broke, the person left holding the larger piece got his or her wish. (This was called the "lucky break.")

Ancient people believed that evil spirits were everywhere, waiting for opportunities to harm people. The spirits were attracted particularly to weddings, where it was easy for them to spot two happy young people—the bride and the groom—and give them bad luck. There was, however, a way to outsmart the evil spirits. Friends of the bride dressed exactly as she was dressed, and friends of the groom dressed exactly as he was dressed. That way, the evil spirits wouldn't know who was getting married.

B Match each ancient belief with one of the modern superstitions or customs listed below. Write the number of your answer on the line.

In the United States today:

_____ a. At weddings, the bridesmaids—friends of the bride—usually wear identical dresses, and the groomsmen—friends of the groom—usually wear identical suits.

_____ b. When people talk about their good fortune, they knock on wood to protect their good luck.

_____ c. It is considered unlucky to spill salt, and people who spill it immediately throw a little of the spilled salt over their left shoulder to reverse the bad luck. (They throw the salt over their *left* shoulder because primitive people believed that evil spirits were always on the left.)

_____ d. People believe it is bad luck if a black cat crosses their path.

_____ e. People bake birthday cakes and top them with candles. The person celebrating a birthday tries to blow out all the candles in one breath for good luck.

_____ f. People are afraid to walk under a ladder.

_____ g. After eating a chicken, people dry the collarbone, which is called the "wishbone." Two people make a wish and pull on the bone. After the bone breaks, the person holding the larger piece gets his or her wish.

UNIT 10

1 PRE-READING

A The title of the next story is "Flight 5390." What do you think happened to Flight 5390? With a partner or in a small group, make up a story and write it down. Be sure to include:

1. the name of the airline
2. the month and year of the flight
3. where the flight took off

4. where the flight landed
5. how many passengers were on the flight
6. how the pilot was injured

B Read the story on the next page. Compare your story with the true story.

Flight 5390

On a beautiful June morning in 1990, Nigel Ogden stood at the door of a British Airways airplane. "Good morning! Good morning!" he said to the passengers as they boarded the plane. Nigel was a flight attendant, and he was working on a 7:30 a.m. flight from Birmingham, England, to Malaga, Spain. He was 36 years old, and he loved his job.

At 7:30, Nigel strapped himself into his seat next to Simon, another flight attendant. They talked for a few minutes about rugby,[1] Nigel's favorite sport. He not only watched the games, but also played on weekends.

The plane took off, and thirteen minutes later, it was at 17,300 feet. Nigel walked into the cockpit and asked the pilot and copilot if they would like some tea. He was walking out of the cockpit when there was an enormous explosion.

Nigel turned around and saw that the pilot's windshield was completely gone, and the wind was sucking the pilot out through the window. He was already halfway out. Nigel grabbed the pilot's legs and tried to pull him back into the plane, but he couldn't; the wind was too strong. So the pilot stayed where he was—half in and half out of the plane.

The copilot was luckier; the windshield on his side was still there. He looked over at Nigel, who was holding on to the pilot's legs. "Is he OK?" he shouted over the roar of the wind. "I don't know," Nigel shouted back.

The wind was sucking everything out of the plane. Water bottles, sunglasses, hats, and books flew past Nigel's head and out the window. Nigel could feel the wind sucking him out of the plane, too. Just then Simon walked into the cockpit. He grabbed Nigel's pants belt to stop him from slipping further and strapped him into the pilot's seat. Then Simon left to take care of the passengers.

Thanks to Nigel's weekend rugby games, his arms were strong, and he was able to hold on to the pilot. But his arms were getting tired. How much longer could he hold on? He tried to see the pilot's face, but he couldn't; it was covered with blood. "We have to let him go," the copilot said. "No," Nigel said. "Maybe he's alive. I can't let him go."

While Nigel was trying to hold on to the pilot, the copilot was trying to get control of the plane. He dived down to 11,000 feet, where there was more oxygen. Then he called air-traffic control and asked for an airport with a long runway. The plane was heavy with fuel, and he was afraid it would go off the end of the runway when it landed. Air-traffic control told him that the nearest airport was in Southampton, England, and that it had only a medium-sized runway. He had to land there.

In the back of the plane, the eighty-one passengers were silent. A man with a baby on his knee said quietly, "We're going to die." "No, we aren't," Simon answered. But he thought the man was probably right.

A few minutes later, the copilot landed the plane, and it was a completely smooth landing. The plane stopped three-quarters of the way down the runway.

The passengers left the plane, and paramedics rushed in to take care of the pilot. He was covered in blood from a cut on his head, and he had a broken wrist and thumb. Otherwise, he was fine. He remembered nothing of the eighteen minutes he had been outside the plane, so he had probably been unconscious. Nigel ran out onto the front steps of the plane and shouted, "He's alive!" Then he sat down on the steps and cried.

Why had the pilot's windshield blown out? The day before, a mechanic had replaced the windshield. When he put the new windshield in, he had used bolts that were too small.

That afternoon, all but six of the passengers went on to Spain. Nigel went to see them at the departure gate. When the passengers saw Nigel, they all turned to him and applauded. Then they boarded the plane to Spain.

---

1 Rugby is a sport played in Great Britain. It is similar to American football.

2 VOCABULARY

LOOKING AT THE STORY

Match the words with the people, things, or actions in the picture. Write the numbers of your answers on the lines.

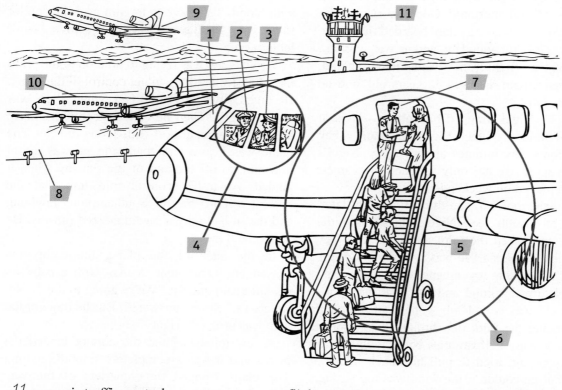

<u>11</u> **a.** air-traffic control

_____ **b.** boarding

_____ **c.** cockpit

_____ **d.** copilot

_____ **e.** flight attendant

_____ **f.** landing

_____ **g.** passenger

_____ **h.** pilot

_____ **i.** runway

_____ **j.** takeoff

_____ **k.** windshield

LOOKING AT WORDS THAT GO TOGETHER

Some words in English go together. For example, if you ask people to complete this phrase: "_a loud _____,_" most people will say "noise." The words _loud_ and _noise_ go together.

A Ask native speakers of English to complete the following sentences and phrases, which contain words from the story. Write their answers on the lines.

1. the _roar_ of the _____

2. At the hardware store, I bought _nuts_ and _____ .

3. Be careful! Don't _slip_ on the _____ .

4. _Strap_ yourself _into_ your _____ .

5. The pilot made a _smooth_ _____ .

6. There's always a lot of traffic during _rush_ _____ .

B Report the answers back to the class. You and your classmates will probably have many of the same answers. When you learn these new words, learn the words that often go with them, too.

3 COMPREHENSION / READING SKILLS

FORMING MENTAL IMAGES AS YOU READ

The story of Flight 5390 could be a movie with four scenes.

Read the sentences below. They describe the four scenes in the movie. One description in each scene is incorrect. Cross out the description that is *not* correct.

Scene 1: At the airport in Birmingham

a. It is early in the morning on a sunny day.

b. Passengers are boarding a British Airways plane.

c. The passengers are wearing summer clothes.

~~d. A female flight attendant in her mid-twenties is standing at the door of the airplane.~~

Scene 2: In the cockpit

a. The pilot's windshield is missing.

b. The pilot is half in and half out of the airplane.

c. A male flight attendant is sitting in the pilot's seat, holding on to the pilot's legs.

d. Another male flight attendant is sitting in the copilot's seat. He is flying the airplane.

e. Wind is roaring through the cockpit.

f. Water bottles, books, and sunglasses are going out through the pilot's window.

Scene 3: In the back of the airplane

a. There are eighty-one passengers, all strapped in their seats.

b. Some of the passengers are screaming and crying.

c. A flight attendant is talking to a male passenger who is holding a baby on his lap.

Scene 4: At the airport in Southampton

a. The airplane has just landed and is at the end of the runway.

b. Passengers are going down the stairs.

c. Paramedics are going up the stairs.

d. The pilot is half in and half out of the window.

UNDERSTANDING SEQUENCE

Complete the timeline of events of Flight 5390 with the events listed in the box. Write each event in the correct place in the timeline.

> Copilot calls air-traffic control; asks for emergency landing.
>
> Passengers leave the plane; paramedics rush in.
>
> Plane takes off.
>
> Explosion at front of plane; pilot's windshield blows out.
>
> Air-traffic control tells copilot to land at Southampton airport.

7:00 a.m.   Passengers board plane.

7:30   _____

7:43   _____

7:45   Copilot dives to 11,000 feet.

7:46   _____

7:49   _____

8:01   Plane lands.

8:02   _____

8:07   Paramedics take care of the pilot.

4 DISCUSSION

The passengers on Flight 5390 had a terrifying experience, and the plane had to make an emergency landing.

A In a small group, tell about a bad experience you have had with flying. For example, maybe you missed your flight; your flight was canceled; there was bad weather during your flight; or your luggage was lost.

B In a small group, tell about a bad experience you had while traveling by car, train, or bus. For example, maybe you had a flat tire; the weather was bad; the train was late; or the bus was crowded.

C In a small group, decide which is the most dangerous way to travel—flying, driving, taking a train, or taking a bus. Then check the Key on page 138 to see if you were right.

5 WRITING

A Imagine this: You are Nigel Ogden, a flight attendant on Flight 5390. Investigators have asked you to write a report about what happened on the flight. Write a report. Tell what you saw, what you heard, and what you did. For example, you might begin:

At 7:00 a.m., I went to the door of the plane and greeted passengers as they boarded. Then, around 7:30, I strapped myself into my seat for takeoff. . . .

B Write the story that you told in Exercise 4A.

Some people are afraid to fly. They think that it is risky, and they believe that the odds of dying in a plane crash are high.

A Are you afraid of flying? Put an **X** on the line near your answer.

I'm **very**
afraid of flying.   •   I'm **not at all**
afraid of flying.

B The graphic below shows the odds of dying from various causes in the United States. Match the odds with the causes. Take a guess, and write the letter of your answer on the line.

467 / 1 _____

1,000 / 1

1,656 / 1 _____

2,000 / 1

3,000 / 1

4,000 / 1

5,000 / 1

157,300 / 1 _____

1 million / 1

2 million / 1

2.3 million / 1 _____

3 million / 1

4 million / 1

5 million / 1

6 million / 1

7 million / 1   **7 million / 1** _____

8 million / 1

a. plane crash

b. falling down stairs

c. heart disease

d. storm

e. all accidents and injuries

C Check the Key on page 138 to see if you guessed right. Has learning about the odds of dying from various causes changed your feelings about flying? Put your **X** on the line again.

I'm **very**
afraid of flying.   •   I'm **not at all**
afraid of flying.

D Read what an expert has to say about risk.

Some people are afraid of flying, so they don't travel by plane. Instead, they travel by train, bus, or car. Are they reducing the risk of dying or getting injured during their trip? David Ropeik says they probably aren't; in fact, they may be making a riskier choice.

Dr. Ropeik works at Harvard University in the United States. He is an expert in risks—that is, he studies what is dangerous and what is not. Flying, he says, is not very dangerous. Why, then, are so many people afraid of flying?

Dr. Ropeik has an explanation. He says that, in general, we are afraid of risks that:

- we can't control.
- could kill us in a particularly awful way.
- are man-made.
- we often see in the news.

Flying is the type of risk that makes us fearful. That explains *why* many of us are afraid of flying. But it doesn't mean we *should* be afraid.

"We worry about the wrong things," Dr. Ropeik says, "and that's what's really dangerous." While we're busy worrying about imaginary dangers—like flying in an airplane—we're not protecting ourselves against real dangers. In the United States, someone dies in a car crash every thirteen minutes, yet 13 percent of Americans don't wear seat belts. Heart disease is the leading cause of death in the United States, yet 33 percent of Americans are obese. Lung cancer is the second leading cause of death in the United States, yet 17 percent of Americans smoke.

In the United States, flying is relatively safe: The risk of dying in a plane crash is only 1 in 7 million. Heart disease, however, is a real danger: The risk of dying of heart disease is about 1 in 400. So which should we fear more—an airplane trip or the big, juicy hamburger with fries that we eat before getting on the plane? Dr. Ropeik thinks there is more danger in the hamburger than there is in the plane trip.

What would Dr. Ropeik say to someone who is considering driving hundreds, perhaps thousands of miles to avoid flying? "Get on the plane," he would probably say. "It really is safe."

E Has the reading changed your feelings about flying? Put an **X** on the line again.

I'm **very** afraid of flying. •• I'm **not at all** afraid of flying.

F In this Challenge section, you put an **X** on the line three times. Did you put your **X** in the same place all three times, or did you move it? On the lines below, explain why your feelings about flying did or did not change.

_____

_____

_____

_____

_____

_____

1 PRE-READING

Look at the picture and think about these questions. Discuss your answers with your classmates.

1. Do you like stories that scare you?

2. Do you know a scary story? Tell it to your classmates.

3. Is your scary story true or not true? How do you know?

A Killer in the Back Seat

Have you heard this story?

At 2:00 a.m., a young nurse left the hospital where she worked, got into her car, and headed for home. On the way home, she stopped at an all-night store for milk. As she was paying for the milk, the cashier reminded her to be careful. "You know about the murder, don't you?" he asked her.

Of course she knew about the murder. A few weeks before, a local woman who had been driving alone late at night had been murdered. The police were still looking for the killer.

The woman got into her car, locked the car doors, and pulled out of the parking lot. A man in a pickup truck pulled out right behind her and followed her, staying just inches from her rear bumper. Every few seconds, he turned on his bright lights.

Her heart pounding, the woman sped home. When she pulled into her driveway, the man in the pickup truck pulled in right behind her. The woman threw open the car door and ran toward her house. Halfway to the front door, she fainted.

When the woman came to, she saw a man kneeling beside her. He was the man in the pickup truck! "It's OK," the man said, and pointed to another man lying on the ground nearby. The man's hands and feet were tied.

"I'm the one who followed you," the stranger said. "I had just pulled into the parking lot of the all-night store when I saw a man get into your car and crouch down in the back seat. Then you came out of the store and got into the car. There was nothing I could do but follow you. I turned on my bright lights every time the guy popped up from the back seat to let him know I was behind you. When you got out of your car, he tried to run away. I hit him with my tire iron. He had a knife, but he didn't get a chance to use it. The police are on their way here. I'm sorry I scared you."

"That's all right," the woman said. "That's all right."

It is a frightening story, and it could have happened. It *could* have happened, but it didn't. It is an urban legend.

Urban legends, like ancient legends, are stories that many people tell one another. They are called "urban" legends because they often take place in or near cities.

Urban legends are not true stories. Many people believe they are true, however, because they are very realistic. In fact, sometimes urban legends are so believable, they are picked up by the news media and reported as news. If urban legends sometimes fool even experienced reporters, how can the average person know if a story is true or if it is an urban legend?

An urban legend always has this characteristic: It is a friend-of-a-friend story. Someone telling an urban legend might begin, "This really happened to my dentist's son-in-law," or "Did you hear what happened to my neighbor's cousin?" But if you try to trace the story back to the son-in-law or the cousin, the trail always evaporates.

Another characteristic of an urban legend is that it is rich in detail. An urban legend always includes the names of local people, local places, and local streets. For example, a person telling the story of the killer in the back seat would never begin, "A young nurse left the hospital where she worked." Instead, the story would begin something like this:

"You know Mr. Soto—the man who lives next door to my cousin? Well, this really happened to one of his nieces. She works at Community Hospital. Anyway, last week she was on her way home from work, about two o'clock in the morning, and..."

As an urban legend moves from person to person, and from city to city, the details of the story change. Mr. Soto's niece becomes Mrs. Alberti's daughter-in-law. She isn't a nurse at Community Hospital; she's a waitress at the Coffee Cup Café. The story, though, remains essentially the same, no matter how far it travels. And these days, urban legends do indeed travel far.

In the past, urban legends spread by word of mouth—one person told the story to another person. Now urban legends spread by phone,

continued ▶

e-mail, and social media. They spread to every corner of the world, and with lightning speed.

One final story:

This book has magical powers. On the front cover of the book, you will see its title: *TRUE STORIES*. If you put your hand on the word *TRUE* and make a wish, your wish will come true. One student put her hand on the word and wished for a lot of money. The next day, she won the lottery—$6 million. This really happened. The student who won the lottery is the sister of my nephew's girlfriend.

2 VOCABULARY

LOOKING AT THE STORY

Complete the sentences with the words below.

came to	fool	rear bumper
detail	headed	reminded
evaporates	realistic	spread by word of mouth

1. The cashier wanted the nurse to remember that a woman had been killed. He ___*reminded*___ her about the murder.

2. After the woman bought milk, she went in the direction of her house. She _____ for home.

3. The man in the pickup truck was behind the woman's car. He stayed just inches from her _____.

4. The woman fainted. A few minutes later, she woke up. When she _____, she saw a man kneeling beside her.

5. Urban legends are believable stories that could happen in real life. Urban legends are very _____.

6. The media sometimes make mistakes, and they report urban legends as news. Urban legends _____ even experienced reporters.

7. Someone telling an urban legend might begin, "Did you hear what happened to my neighbor's cousin?" But if you try to follow the story back to the cousin, the trail disappears. The trail _____ because the story isn't true.

8. Urban legends always include the names of local people, places, and streets; they are rich in _____.

9. Urban legends _____—one person tells the story to another person.

LOOKING AT SPECIAL EXPRESSIONS

Find the best way to complete each sentence. Write the letter of your answer on the line.

to pull into = to enter (while driving a car)

1. The woman sped home and __*b*__

2. It's going to rain; you'd better _____

3. We were really hungry, so we _____

    a. pull the car into the garage.

    b. pulled into her driveway.

    c. pulled into the drive-through lane of a fast-food restaurant.

to let someone know = to tell someone; to inform someone

4. The man in the pickup truck turned on his bright lights _____

5. If you need any help fixing your car, _____

6. We've changed the time of the meeting; _____

    d. please let everyone know it's at one o'clock, not two.

    e. just let me know; I've worked as a mechanic.

    f. to let the man in the back seat know he saw him.

no matter how = it makes no difference

7. No matter how far an urban legend travels, _____

8. No matter how much he eats, _____

9. No matter how long it takes, _____

    g. he doesn't gain weight because he exercises a lot.

    h. we have to finish this job.

    i. the story remains essentially the same.

3 COMPREHENSION/READING SKILLS

UNDERSTANDING THE MAIN IDEAS

Check (✓) six correct ways to complete the sentence.

Urban legends...

☐ a. are not true.

☐ b. are ancient.

☐ c. often take place in or near cities.

☐ d. are realistic.

☐ e. are friend-of-a-friend stories.

☐ f. have many details.

☐ g. always include the names of famous people.

☐ h. remain essentially the same, no matter how far they travel.

UNDERSTANDING CAUSE AND EFFECT

Find the best way to complete each sentence. Write the letter of your answer on the line.

1. Untrue stories that people tell one another are called urban legends __e__

2. Urban legends are sometimes reported as news _____

3. A story that begins, "This really happened to my neighbor's cousin" might be an urban legend _____

4. Urban legends move from city to city, yet still include the names of local people and local places _____

5. These days, urban legends travel fast _____

a. because the storytellers change the details to fit the city.

b. because they spread not only by word of mouth, but also by phone, e-mail, and social media.

c. because it has a friend-of-a-friend beginning.

d. because they are very realistic.

e. because they often take place in or near cities.

4 DISCUSSION

A Below are the topics of some popular urban legends. Have you heard a story about any of these topics? If so, tell the class the story you heard. Include any details you remember.

• a restaurant that serves dog (or cat or rat) meat

• a mouse in a can of soda

• a young woman who is kidnapped from a dressing room in a department store (She falls through a trap door.)

• looking into a mirror and seeing ghosts or a woman with no eyes

• a poisonous snake in an imported blanket (or sweater or coat)

• a carpet installer who sees a bump in a carpet and finds a missing pet canary (or hamster or gerbil)

• a hitchhiker who disappears

• a female hitchhiker with hairy arms or the feet of a horse

• tourists in Australia who put a coat on a kangaroo

• a female insect that goes into someone's ear

• a grandmother who dies on a family vacation

• spiders in a cactus or yucca plant

• a stolen kidney

• stolen children

• a babysitter who gets a phone call from a killer

• alligators in the sewer system of a big city

B In a small group, invent an urban legend. Begin your story, "This really happened to…" One at a time, your classmates will add a sentence to the story. Before your classmates say their own sentences, they will repeat the previous sentence. The last student in the group provides the ending to the story.

5 WRITING

Write an urban legend. You can write one of the stories your classmates told in Exercise 4A, the one your classmates invented in Exercise 4B, or one of your own. Make it a "friend-of-a-friend" story, include details, and mention the names of local people, places, and streets. Here is what one student wrote.

A friend of my mom's friend is a taxi driver in São Paulo, Brazil. Her name is Monica. Like many taxi drivers, Monica has amazing stories. The story I'm going to tell you now is true. This really happened to Monica.

Monica was driving her taxi home after a long day. At exactly midnight, she was passing Primavera Cemetery and saw a woman in a black dress holding her arm out for a taxi. She stopped the taxi, and the woman got in the back seat. She introduced herself as Carol. Carol said that her car had broken down. Carol asked Monica to drive her to her parents' house on Boa Vista Street. During the whole trip, Carol asked weird questions about death. Sometimes Monica looked back at Carol just to see her face, but it was too dark and she couldn't see it. Monica also started to smell flowers in her car. It was the kind of smell that reminds you of a cemetery.

When they got to the home of Carol's parents, Carol asked Monica to wait while she went inside to get some money. Monica waited fifteen minutes. Then she went to the door and knocked three times. A man about 50 years old, wearing pajamas, answered the door. Monica said, "I'm waiting for Carol, your daughter." The man's eyes filled with tears. "Is this a bad joke?" he said. "I did have a daughter named Carol, but her funeral was at Primavera Cemetery ten years ago today. She died in a taxi accident."

CHALLENGE

Jan Harold Brunvand is an expert in urban legends. He has been collecting them for years. The following are seven stories that Dr. Brunvand has determined are urban legends—that is, they are stories that many people believe are true but are not true. There is also one story that *is* true.

A Read the eight stories.

1

An old woman drove her car—a Mercedes—into a crowded parking lot. She drove around for a while, looking for a parking space, and finally found one. Just as she was about to pull into the space, a young man in a shiny red sports car sped around the woman and pulled into the space. He got out of his car and smiled at the woman. "Sorry," he said. "But that's what you can do when you're young and fast."

The old woman pushed the accelerator of her Mercedes to the floor and crashed into the sports car. Then she put her car in reverse, backed up, and crashed into it again. The young man rushed over to the old woman. "What are you doing?" he yelled. The old woman handed him her insurance card and smiled. "That's what you can do when you're old and rich," she said.

2

During World War II, a German woman wrote a letter to relatives in the United States. In her letter, the woman said that she was fine. She suggested that her American cousin, Johnny, steam the stamp off the envelope to add to his stamp collection.

The woman's relatives were puzzled. There was no Johnny in the family, nor were there any stamp collectors. The relatives realized that this was a clue. They steamed the stamp off the envelope and found that under the stamp, the German woman had written in tiny letters: "Help us. We are starving."

3

Two pilots were flying an airplane with 150 passengers. The copilot left the cockpit to use the lavatory and didn't return. A long time passed. Concerned, the pilot decided to check on the copilot. He put the plane on autopilot and stepped out of the cockpit. Just then, the plane hit a pocket of turbulence, and the door to the cockpit slammed shut and locked. In order to get back into the cockpit, the two pilots had to smash the door with an ax in front of the terrified passengers.

4

A woman bought her boyfriend a small cell phone. She wrapped the gift and put it on a table. The next day, all that remained of the present was torn wrapping paper. The woman searched her apartment for the phone, but found nothing. She decided to call the phone and heard it ringing where her dog was sleeping. At first she thought the dog was lying on the phone, but then realized that the phone was ringing *inside* the dog. She rushed the dog to the vet, who determined that the dog had indeed swallowed the phone. The vet told the woman that her dog was in no danger and told her to let nature take its course. The phone emerged from the dog the next day in perfect working order.

5

A woman was shopping at a large department store. She put her purse down for a minute, and it was stolen.

A few hours later, the woman was back home when the phone rang. It was a man who said he was the department store manager. He told the woman her purse was found in the store and that she could pick it up at his office.

When the woman arrived at the store, her purse was not there, and the manager knew nothing about the phone call. The woman raced home and found her keys in the lock of her front door. When she went inside, she discovered that everything of value was gone.

6

A young woman who lived alone had a large dog—a Doberman—for protection. One day, the woman came home from work and found the Doberman choking. The woman brought her dog to the vet.

The vet examined the dog briefly and then told the woman to go back home. The vet wanted to keep the dog for a few tests and would call the woman later.

When the woman returned home, the phone was ringing. It was the vet. "Get out of your apartment immediately!" the vet said. "Go to a neighbor's and call the police!"

The vet had found two human fingers in the Doberman's throat. When the police arrived at the woman's apartment, they found an unconscious man in a closet. The man was bleeding and missing two fingers.

7

A man ate some chocolate chip cookies at a small shop in a shopping mall. He liked the cookies so much that he phoned the company the next day and asked for the recipe. A company representative told the man he could not have the recipe; it was a secret. "Well," the man asked, "would you let me buy the recipe?" The representative said he could. "How much?" the man asked. "Nine-fifty," was the reply. "Just put the charge on my credit card," the man said.

When the man received his credit card statement, he found out that he had paid $950 for the chocolate chip cookie recipe. The man tried to get his money back, but he couldn't, so he decided he was going to have $950 worth of fun. He e-mailed the recipe to everyone he knew and asked them to pass it on to someone else. Now almost everyone in the country has the "secret" recipe.

8

A businessman was riding the New York subway home from work. The man standing next to him kept bumping into him. The businessman became suspicious and patted his back pocket. His wallet was missing! The businessman grabbed the man and shook him. "Give me the wallet!" he demanded. The man handed him a wallet.

When the businessman returned home that evening, he found his wallet on the dresser in his bedroom. The wallet in his pocket belonged to the man on the subway.

B Which seven stories do you think are urban legends? Which story do you think is true? Circle the number of the true story. Then check the Key on page 138 to see if you guessed right.

UNIT 12

1 PRE-READING

A Think about these questions. Discuss your answers with your classmates.

1. What do you think is the best job?

2. What do you think is the worst job?

3. In your country, which jobs do people think are good jobs?

4. If you are working, why did you choose your job?

5. If you are in school, what job are you preparing for? Why did you choose that job?

6. What job do you want to be doing five years from now?

7. When you were a child, what job did you want to have when you grew up?

B People sometimes say, "You can be anything you want to be." Is that true? Put an **X** on the line near your answer.

Yes, it's true. •• No, it's not true.

C Explain your answer in a small group.

How You Finish

Gabe Sonnier had been the custodian at an elementary school in Louisiana for four years. One day he was cleaning a classroom when the school's principal dropped by to see him. "Do you have a minute?" the principal asked.

"Sure," Gabe said as he picked a piece of paper up from the floor.

"Being a custodian is a good job, and it's an honest living," the principal began. "But I think you'd benefit the students more as an educator. I'd rather see you grading papers than picking them up."

"What do you mean?" Gabe asked.

"I think you're a smart man, with unlimited potential. And I know you love children. You should be a teacher."

Later Gabe thought about the principal's words: *You're a smart man with unlimited potential. You love children. You should be a teacher.* It was true that Gabe loved children. Maybe he was smart—when he was a boy in school, he got good grades. And he wanted to be a teacher very much. But how could he be a teacher? He didn't have a university education. And did he really have unlimited potential? Wasn't it too late now to change his future?

Gabe had never planned to be a custodian. When he was 20 years old, he was a university student, studying electrical engineering. Then his parents got divorced, and his father left. Gabe's mother cleaned houses for a living, but there wasn't enough money to support Gabe and his four brothers and sisters. So Gabe quit school and went to work. He worked in construction, at a grocery store, and at a sawmill. Then he got the job as the custodian at the elementary school. He planned to work five, maybe ten years as a custodian. Then he would look for something else.

Fifteen years after his talk with the principal, Gabe was still the school's custodian, with his own family to support. He had a wife and two sons who were both university students. He couldn't quit his job and go back to school—his family needed his salary. But the principal's words had planted a seed in Gabe's heart and mind.

As the school's custodian, Gabe sometimes came into a classroom during school hours to clean up a spill. He often looked at the teacher and thought, "I would like to be that teacher." But to be a teacher, Gabe needed a university degree. He was 39 years old. Could he be a student again at his age? Could he take classes at the university *and* work? He decided to try it.

Every morning Gabe cleaned the elementary school from 5 a.m. to 7 a.m. Then he drove to the university and attended classes all day. After his last class, he went home, took a nap, and had dinner with his family. Around 8 p.m., he went back to the elementary school and cleaned until midnight. When he got home, he studied for an hour or two. Then he slept for a few hours. At 5 a.m. he was back at the elementary school. That was his schedule for eight years.

At age 47, Gabe graduated from the university and began looking for a teaching job. There was an opening at the elementary school where he was a custodian—the school needed a third-grade teacher. Gabe applied for the job and got it. After 27 years as a custodian, he was a teacher! But he wasn't finished with his education. He wanted a master's degree.

For the next six years, Gabe took online courses in the evening and got his master's degree. Then there was another opening at the elementary school—the school needed a new principal. Gabe applied for the job and got it. Gabe became the principal of the school where he used to be the custodian.

Most of the children at the elementary school are poor. It will not be easy for them to make their dreams come true. It wasn't easy for Gabe, either. He tells the children, "Where you begin is not important. What *is* important? How you finish."

2 VOCABULARY

LOOKING AT THE STORY

Complete the sentences with the words below.

attended	dropped by	online	support
benefit	grading	opening	unlimited potential
Do you have a minute?	master's degree	sawmill	used to

1. The principal didn't make an appointment to talk to Gabe. He _____*dropped by*_____ when Gabe was cleaning a classroom.

2. The principal knew that Gabe was working and didn't have much time to talk. So he began the conversation by saying, "_____."

3. Gabe helped the students by cleaning the classrooms. But the principal thought Gabe could help the students more by teaching them. He said, "I think you'd _____ the students more as an educator."

4. The principal thought that Gabe had many possibilities in his future. He thought Gabe could do almost anything. "You have _____," he told Gabe.

5. Gabe's mother needed money to buy food and clothes for his brothers and sisters. She needed money to pay the rent, too. Gabe went to work so that he could help _____ his family.

6. After he quit school, Gabe had several jobs. At one job, he cut trees into pieces to make wood. The job at the _____ was difficult and dangerous.

7. Gabe was at the university every day from 9 a.m. to 4 p.m. He _____ classes regularly.

8. The elementary school where Gabe was the custodian needed a third-grade teacher. When Gabe heard there was an _____, he applied for the job.

9. When Gabe became a teacher, he read his students' tests and homework. He spent a lot of time _____ papers.

10. Gabe was a university graduate, but he wanted more education. He wanted a _____.

11. The local university didn't have the classes Gabe needed for his master's degree. But another university had classes on the Internet, so Gabe took courses _____.

12. Gabe doesn't clean classrooms anymore; he has a different job. He is the principal of the school where he _____ be the custodian.

LOOKING AT A NEW CONTEXT

A Give examples to show you understand the meanings of the new words. You do not need to write complete sentences.

Name...

1. a school that you've attended. _____

2. a change that would benefit a lot of people. _____

3. someone you would welcome into your home if they dropped by. _____

4. the best grade teachers can give students in your country. _____

5. something you often do online. _____

6. a job you would apply for if there were an opening. _____

7. a person who you think has unlimited potential. _____

8. something you used to do but never do now. _____

B In a small group, take turns reading your answers aloud. Ask your classmates questions about their answers.

3 COMPREHENSION / READING SKILLS

UNDERSTANDING THE MAIN IDEAS

A Imagine this: Two people are having a conversation about the story. Speaker A has not read the story and is asking questions about it. Speaker B has read the story and is answering the questions. Write the missing words on the lines.

1. **Speaker A:** What's the story about?

    Speaker B: It's about the _____*principal*_____ of an elementary school in Louisiana.

2. **Speaker A:** What's special about him?

    Speaker B: He used to be the _____ at the school. He did that for _____ years.

3. **Speaker A:** And somebody gave him the job of principal?

    Speaker B: Not exactly. First, he had to get a university _____.

4. **Speaker A:** Why didn't he get his degree when he was younger?

    Speaker B: He _____ school when he was 20 and went to work.

5. **Speaker A:** Why?

    Speaker B: His parents got _____, and he had to help his mom support his brothers and sisters.

6. **Speaker A:** So he went back to school later and got his degree?

   Speaker B: Yes, but it wasn't easy—he continued to work as a custodian and took classes at the _____. It took him _____ years to finish his degree.

7. **Speaker A:** And then he got the job as a principal?

   Speaker B: No, he got a job as a _____ at the school. Then he took _____ courses to get his _____ degree. That took him six years. *Then* he got the job as principal.

B Read the conversation with a partner. If you are Speaker B, you can read the answers above, or you can answer in your own words.

UNDERSTANDING SUPPORTING DETAILS

Read each sentence on the left. Which sentence on the right gives you more information? Write the letter of your answer on the line.

_c_ 1. Gabe was a custodian.

____ 2. He thought about the principal's words.

____ 3. When Gabe was 20, he was a university student.

____ 4. He quit college and went to work.

____ 5. He had his own family to support.

____ 6. There was an opening at the elementary school.

a. The school needed a third-grade teacher.

b. You're a smart man with unlimited potential. You love children. You should be a teacher.

c. He cleaned the classrooms at an elementary school in Louisiana.

d. He was studying electrical engineering.

e. He worked in construction, at a grocery store, and at a sawmill.

f. He had a wife and two sons.

4 DISCUSSION

Gabe Sonnier had a goal: He wanted to get a university degree and become a teacher. So he made a plan to reach his goal. He decided to clean the school early in the morning and late at night, and take classes at the university during the day.

A What about you? Do you have a goal? How will you reach your goal? In the chart below, write your goal and how you plan to reach it.

My Goal	My Plan to Reach My Goal
I want to . . .	*I will . . .*

B Share your goal and your plan in a small group.

5 WRITING

The story "How You Finish" begins with an anecdote. An anecdote is a short story about a real event. It is usually interesting or funny. The anecdote in the story "How You Finish" is about Gabe's conversation with the school principal.

A Read the anecdote on page 97 again. (It is the first five paragraphs of the story.) As you read, notice that the anecdote:

- begins with background information: *Gabe Sonnier had been the custodian at an elementary school in Louisiana for four years.*

- describes where Gabe was and what he was doing when the event happened: *One day he was cleaning a classroom when the school's principal dropped by to see him.*

- includes direct quotes, for example: *"Do you have a minute?" the principal asked.*

B On your own paper, write an anecdote from your own life. Remember to:

- begin with background information.

- describe where you were and what you were doing when the event happened.

- include direct quotes.

Here is what one student wrote.

Death by Flea Powder

When my cat gets fleas, I kill the fleas with flea powder. One time I bought flea powder for my cat and left it on the kitchen counter. The days passed, and I didn't use it. I forgot about the flea powder on the counter.

One day my brother-in-law came to my house to help do some work in the yard. He decided to cook something. He went to the kitchen to prepare some meat.

My husband went inside, and he saw the container of flea powder very close to the food. He asked, "Did you put some of this on the food?" My brother-in-law said, "Yes. It's onion powder, right?" My husband said, "Didn't you see the label? There's a cat on the label! It's for cats, not humans!"

Of course, we threw the food away.

CHALLENGE

When he was the custodian at an elementary school, Gabe Sonnier had a conversation with the school's principal. That conversation changed Mr. Sonnier's life.

A The true stories below are based on actual life-changing conversations. Read the stories.

1 The Interview

When I was in my early 30s, I lived in New York City, I was broke, and I really needed a job. One of the big hotels was looking for a sales and marketing director. I applied for the job and got an appointment for an interview.

I bought a nice suit and showed up for the interview with my résumé in my hand and a smile on my face. Halfway through the interview, the interviewer stopped and said, "I don't think you really want this job." The interview was over.

I remember walking down the street in tears after the interview. But then I realized the interviewer was right: I didn't really want that job, and I didn't want to go to any more interviews. I didn't want to live in New York anymore, either.

2 The Smart One

I was 14 years old and attending a private school. It was a good school, but not a great school. My younger brother had just won a scholarship to a much better private school.

I was at a sports event with my father at my school, and he got into a conversation with another parent. "Congratulations on your smart children," the other parent said.

My father looked at me and said, "Actually, his younger brother is the smart one." I remember that the other parent gasped with surprise and said, "Oh."

My father died at the age of 51, when I was 29. It is shattering how one comment can change your life.

3 The Drop-Out

When I was a junior in college, my grades were really bad. So I decided to drop out of school. At my next meeting with my academic advisor, I told him my decision.

"Why are you going to drop out?" my advisor asked.

I listed all my reasons. My advisor listened without saying anything. When I finished talking, he repeated my reasons one by one. He didn't give me advice, and he didn't give me a pep talk.

After our meeting, I felt embarrassed. I realized that I had used my reasons for quitting school to convince myself I was doing the right thing. But my reasons sounded foolish when my advisor said them.

4 "Someday You'll Thank Me"

Ever since I was a little kid, I dreamed of being an officer in the U.S. Army. So when I was a senior in high school, I decided to apply to the United States Military Academy. I asked my favorite teacher to write a letter of recommendation. He told me often that I was a born leader, and he had been in the Army himself. But when I went to his classroom to pick up the letter, he told me he wouldn't write it.

"This isn't a game, Sara," he told me. "To protect our country, you need to be strong. The Army is no place for a woman."

"But you told me I was a born leader," I said.

"You are!" he replied. "You'll probably be president of your own company one day! But you don't belong in the military. Trust me. Someday you'll thank me for not writing that letter."

I was shocked. I walked out of his classroom without saying a word.

5 The Fence

When I was a boy, I liked to help my father do jobs around the house. One day we were painting a fence together when I asked him, "Why does the back of the fence have to look as good as the front? No one will ever know it's not as good."

My father said, "*You* will know."

B How does each story continue? Take a guess. Write the number of the story on the line.

_____ a. I joined the Air Force and became a helicopter pilot. I received several medals during my military service; one of the medals was for heroism.

_____ b. I moved to Mexico and became an artist.

_____ c. When I was in my 20s, I started a technology company, Apple, Inc. I insisted that Apple products be as beautiful on the inside they are on the outside—even the circuit boards, for example, which the customer doesn't see.

_____ d. I studied hard, got into medical school, and became a doctor. Looking back, I think that all the things I have accomplished in my professional life were to prove my father wrong.

_____ e. I finished college and later got a doctorate in International Communication. I became a consultant who helps people in business and government improve their conversation skills.

C Have you ever had a conversation that changed your life in a positive way? In a small group, tell your classmates about the conversation. The group will choose one conversation to act out in front of the class (with the permission of the person who told the story). People in the group will volunteer to play roles. The person who told the story will not take a role. He or she will be the "director."

UNIT 13

1 PRE-READING

A Look at the picture and guess the answers to these questions. Share your guesses with your classmates.

1. In what country was the picture taken?

2. In what year was the picture taken?

B Check the Key on page 138 to see if you guessed correctly. Did the answers surprise you? Do you know anything about the Amish? If you do, tell the class what you know.

The Plain People

It is still dark when Elizabeth wakes up. She gets out of bed and shivers when her feet touch the cold, bare floor. The bedroom is not heated, and it is so cold that she can see her breath. She quickly puts on her long dress, black apron, and black shoes. Then she hurries to the kitchen.

The only light in the kitchen comes from kerosene lamps; Elizabeth's husband lit the lamps earlier, before he went out to milk the cows. Elizabeth puts a few pieces of wood into the stove and starts the fire. Then she begins to prepare a big breakfast for herself, her husband, and their six children. It is the beginning of a typical day for Elizabeth.

Although Elizabeth's day will be typical, her life is certainly not typical of modern life in the United States. Elizabeth belongs to a religious group known as the Amish. The Amish are often called "the plain people" because they live and dress very simply. Their homes have no carpets on the floors, no pictures on the walls, and no soft, comfortable furniture. The men wear dark pants with white or blue shirts, and the women wear long dresses in dark colors. The women never wear makeup or jewelry.

The Amish have a saying: "The old way is the best way." The Amish way of life has not changed much in 300 years. However, the Amish are practical. They have adapted to modern life when necessary, and they do some things in a new way. They have never used electricity from the public grid—and they still don't. But they do use solar and wind power that they generate themselves. They have never driven cars—and they still don't; they ride in buggies pulled by horses. But for safety, they put battery-powered lights on the back of their buggies. One "old way" that has not changed is their language: They still speak German, the language that the first Amish people spoke.

The first Amish people lived in Germany and Switzerland. They were called Amish because their leader was Jacob Amman. The Amish were persecuted in Europe, so around 1720, they came to the New World. They settled in what is now the state of Pennsylvania.

Most of the Amish still live in Pennsylvania, although there are large communities in other states, too. All Amish, no matter where they live, have similar beliefs.

The Amish believe that life in the countryside is best, so many Amish live on farms. Amish farmers do not use modern machinery, yet their farms are successful because the Amish work hard and take good care of their land and animals. Their farms are always small. The Amish think it is wrong to have more land or more money than they need to live. About twenty years ago, some Amish farmers discovered oil on their land. Was there a lot of oil under the ground, or just a little? The Amish farmers didn't want to know. They immediately sold their land and moved away, without telling anyone about the oil. They didn't want to be rich.

The Amish, who are Christians, believe they should follow the peaceful example of Jesus. Amish men will not fight in wars or serve in the army. They will not even wear coats with buttons, because military uniforms often have large gold or silver buttons.

The Amish will not buy insurance of any kind. When there is trouble, they help one another. If an Amish farmer gets sick, relatives and neighbors will milk his cows, plant his fields, and harvest his crops. If a barn burns down, as many as 200 men will come and build a new barn in one day.

The Amish are not allowed to marry people who are not Amish. That has caused a peculiar problem. The 500 or so Amish who came to the New World in the 1700s had about forty last names. The 300,000 Amish who live in the United States today are the descendants of those people—and have the same forty last names. In one school in Pennsylvania, 95 percent of the students—and their teacher—have the last name "Stolzfus." The Amish custom of choosing first names from the Bible adds to the problem. In one small Amish community, there are eleven men named Daniel Miller!

To avoid confusion, the Amish give nicknames to people who have the same name.

continued ▶

Some nicknames have an obvious explanation: "Chicken Dan" sells chickens, for example; "Curly Dan" has curly hair. But what about "Gravy Dan"? How did he get his nickname? At dinner one evening, this Dan wanted to pour some cream into his coffee. He reached for the pitcher of cream but took the pitcher of gravy by mistake, and poured gravy into his coffee. Ever since that evening, his nickname has been "Gravy Dan."

People are curious about the lives of Amish like Elizabeth and Gravy Dan. Every year thousands of tourists visit the part of Pennsylvania where most Amish live. They take pictures of the black buggies and the plain white houses. They watch Amish children as they walk to school and Amish men as they work in their fields. Most Amish are not happy about the tourists, but they tolerate them. Perhaps the Amish understand that the tourists want to experience—at least for a few days—the quieter, simpler Amish way of life.

2 VOCABULARY

LOOKING AT THE STORY

Read each sentence. What is the meaning of the word(s) in *italics*? Circle the letter of the correct answer.

1. Elizabeth shivers when her feet touch the cold, *bare* floor.
   - **(a.)** not covered with a carpet
   - **b.** painted white

2. The Amish don't use electricity from the *public grid*.
   - **a.** the system that carries electricity from a power plant to the customer
   - **b.** the system that provides free electricity to people who cannot pay for it

3. The Amish *were persecuted* in Europe, so they came to the New World.
   - **a.** People were cruel to them.
   - **b.** People were friendly to them.

4. They *settled* in what is now the state of Pennsylvania.
   - **a.** found a new leader
   - **b.** came to live

5. There are large Amish *communities* in other states, too.
   - **a.** groups of people who left their countries because of politics
   - **b.** groups of people who live together

6. All Amish have similar *beliefs*.
   - **a.** objects that are important to them
   - **b.** ideas that they think are true

7. Amish men will not fight in wars. They will not even wear coats with buttons because *military uniforms* often have large gold or silver buttons.
   - **a.** the clothes worn by schoolchildren
   - **b.** the clothes worn by soldiers

8. If an Amish farmer gets sick, relatives and neighbors will *harvest his crops*.
   - **a.** pick the fruit, vegetables, and grain that he grows
   - **b.** bring him the medicine and other things that he needs

9. If a *barn* burns down, as many as 200 men will come and build a new barn in one day.
   - **a.** house that is made of wood and built by hand
   - **b.** building where a farmer keeps his crops and animals

10. The Amish are not allowed to marry people who are not Amish. That has caused a *peculiar* problem.
    a. big
    b. strange

11. A man took a pitcher of *gravy* by mistake and poured it into his coffee.
    a. drink made with lemons and sugar
    b. sauce for meat and potatoes

12. Most Amish are not happy about the tourists, but they *tolerate them*.
    a. allow them to come
    b. make them pay

LOOKING AT A NEW CONTEXT

A **Complete the sentences to show that you understand the meanings of the new words.**

1. A modern-day example of people who are persecuted is _____.

2. If I had to leave my native country, I would settle in _____.

3. A strong belief I have is that _____.

4. Some crops that are harvested near my native city are _____.

5. Something I could never tolerate is _____.

B **In a small group, take turns reading your sentences aloud. Ask your classmates questions about their sentences.**

3 COMPREHENSION / READING SKILLS

UNDERSTANDING THE MAIN IDEAS

What information is *not* in the story? Find that information and cross it out.

1. Elizabeth _____.
   a. sleeps in a bedroom that is not heated
   b. wears a long dress, black apron, and black shoes
   c. ~~has two sons~~
   d. cooks on a wood stove

2. The Amish _____.
   a. are a religious group also called "the plain people"
   b. live and dress very simply
   c. live in California
   d. believe that "the old way is the best way"

3. The first Amish people _____.
   a. spoke French
   b. were led by Jacob Amman
   c. were persecuted in Europe
   d. came to the New World around 1720

4. Some Amish beliefs are: _____.
   a. Life in the countryside is best
   b. Follow the peaceful example of Jesus
   c. Do not buy insurance
   d. Do not work on Mondays

UNDERSTANDING SUPPORTING DETAILS

Find the best way to complete each sentence. Write the letter of your answer on the line.

1. Elizabeth's life is not typical of life in the United States in the twenty-first century. For example, _C_

2. The Amish dress very simply. For example, _____

3. The Amish way of life has not changed much in 300 years. For example, _____

4. The Amish help one another when there is trouble. For example, _____

5. Some nicknames have an obvious explanation. For example, _____

a. they still speak German, the language that the first Amish people spoke.

b. "Chicken Dan" sells chickens and "Curly Dan" has curly hair.

c. she cooks on a wood stove.

d. if a barn burns down, as many as 200 men will come and build a new barn in a day.

e. the women wear long dresses in dark colors.

4 DISCUSSION

A **Think about these questions. Discuss your answers with your classmates.**

1. Amish life is not typical of life in the United States. Are there any small religious groups in your native country who live differently from most people in your country? Tell your classmates about them.

2. Could you live the way the Amish live? For example, could you live without electricity from the power grid and without a car? Explain why or why not.

3. What do you think of the three Amish beliefs listed below? Do you agree with them?
   a. It is wrong to have more money than you need.
   b. Never fight in wars.
   c. Help one another when there is trouble.

4. There is confusion because many Amish have the same last name. Are there some last names that are very common in your native country? What are the names?

5. The Amish give one another nicknames. Do you have a nickname? What is it? Is there a story behind your nickname, like the story of "Gravy Dan"? If you would like, share it with your classmates.

B Think about a religion you know and answer the questions in the chart. Then ask a partner the questions and write your partner's answers in the chart.

	You	Your Partner
1. Which religion do you know the most about?		
2. Where does this religion get its name?		
3. Does this religion have many different groups? If so, what are some of them called?		
4. Is there a holy book? What is it called?		
5. Is any day of the week special? Which day? What do people do on that day?		
6. Which religious holiday is most important? What does the holiday celebrate? What do people do on that holiday?		
7. Are there any rules about food?		
8. Are there any rules about clothing?		
9. What does this religion say happens to people after they die?		

5 WRITING

Write about one of the world's religions. Use the information you wrote in Exercise 4B, or use the information your partner gave you. Here is what one student wrote.

The Mormon religion is a Christian religion that began in 1830. Many Mormons who live in the United States live in the state of Utah.

Mormons have a lot of rules. They don't drink alcohol. They also don't drink coffee, tea, cola, or any drink that has caffeine in it. They must pay the church 10 percent of their income.

In the Mormon church, there are no paid priests or ministers. People volunteer to work as ministers.

Years ago, Mormon men had more than one wife. The Mormons' neighbors and the U.S. government didn't like that, and there was a lot of trouble. But today, the mainstream Mormon church does not allow polygamy.

CHALLENGE

The following are five paragraphs that give more information about Amish life. On page 111, there are five photos.

A Read the paragraphs.

1

When Amish boys are 16, they are given special buggies—called courting buggies—so that they can give girls rides. Some boys add carpeting to their buggies and install stereos. This is actually against the Amish practice of being plain, but adults tolerate it. Some boys even add speedometers so they can see if their buggies can go faster than the average speed of a buggy, which is about 12 miles per hour. One Amish man said, "If you clock a buggy going 15 miles an hour, you can be sure it's a teenage driver!" It is easy to tell a courting buggy from a regular buggy. A regular buggy is covered and looks like a box sitting on wheels, but a courting buggy is open, with no roof.

2

Amish families gather every other Sunday for a worship service that lasts four hours. At an Amish service, the men and women sit separately on wooden benches, and the children sit on benches at the back of the room. (Halfway through the service, the children are given a snack to help them make it to the next meal.) When the service is over, the benches are removed and tables are set up for lunch. The meal is simple but plentiful: There are sandwiches and soup; pickles and pickled beets; bread, butter, and jam; and pies and cake for dessert. Amish services, as well as the meal that follows them, take place not in church buildings—the Amish have no churches—but in people's homes. Anyone on a Sunday drive through the Amish countryside easily can tell where the Sunday services are being held: There will be twenty to thirty-five buggies parked outside the house.

3

The Amish are one of the fastest-growing religious groups in the United States because Amish families have so many children. The average number of children in an Amish family is six, but families with eleven or twelve children are not uncommon. Their growing population has caused a hard-to-solve problem for the Amish. Farmland has become expensive in the United States, and most Amish cannot afford to buy it. As a result, the Amish have too little land for too many people. Some Amish have turned to professions other than farming, with furniture-making being the most popular. Amish-made furniture, which is sold in stores all over the United States, is prized for its quality and durability.

4

In 1985, the movie *Witness* was filmed in Lancaster, Pennsylvania, the home of many Amish. The movie tells the story of an Amish widow who falls in love with a police detective from Philadelphia, played by Harrison Ford. The movie was made without the permission of the Amish, who opposed the film. One scene in the movie particularly offended the Amish. Harrison Ford, dressed in plain clothes, defends his Amish friends in a fistfight. That scene was filmed in front of Zimmerman's Hardware Store, where Amish actually shop. Later, laws were passed in Pennsylvania to protect the Amish from similar movies being made without their permission.

5

The Amish have a saying: "The more you learn, the more you are confused." The Amish believe that education after the eighth grade—that is, after a child is 13 or 14—is unnecessary. That belief caused a serious problem for the Amish in the 1960s. Some states began enforcing laws that required school attendance until age 16, and Amish teenagers had to go to high school. In some cases, police forced Amish children onto school buses while their parents stood by, crying and praying. The Amish did nothing to change the law because they believe that any type of protest—even filing a lawsuit—is wrong. Many non-Amish, however, wanted to help. They formed a group called the National Committee for Amish Religious Freedom, and filed a lawsuit. The case was decided by the U.S. Supreme Court in 1972. The court ruled unanimously that Amish children were exempt from the law and could leave school after the eighth grade. So, today, Amish children are educated in the same way their parents and grandparents were educated— by Amish teachers in one-room schoolhouses. Their formal education stops after eight years.

B Look at the photos. Which photo goes with each paragraph? Write the number of the paragraph on the line below the photo.

a. _____

b. _____

c. _____

d. _____

e. _____

1 PRE-READING

Think about these questions. Discuss your answers with your classmates.

1. Do you know of any old person who died soon after an important event, like a holiday or birthday?

2. Do you think that people can control the time of their own deaths?

Does Death Take a Holiday?

Yinlan looked at the people sitting around the table and smiled contentedly. Everyone in her family was there—her children, her grandchildren, and her new great-grandson, just one month old. Her whole family had come to celebrate the Harvest Moon Festival.

The Harvest Moon Festival is a Chinese celebration. Although Yinlan no longer lived in China—she lived in San Francisco—she and her family still celebrated the Harvest Moon Festival just as Yinlan had in China. At the time of the full moon in August or September, her family gathered at her house for dinner. After dinner, they ate moon cakes, a special round cookie. Then, if the sky was clear, they always walked outside to admire the full moon.

Tonight, there was not a cloud in the sky, and the full moon shone brightly. Yinlan suggested that they all go outside. Her grandson helped her up from her chair. As Yinlan and her grandson walked toward the door, she held on to his arm and leaned against him for support. Yinlan was 86 years old. She had not been well the past few months, and her family noticed that she seemed weak.

Two days after the Harvest Moon Festival, Yinlan died peacefully in her sleep. Her family was sad but, at the same time, grateful. They felt happy that they had been able to celebrate the Harvest Moon Festival with her one last time. They said it seemed that she had waited until after the holiday to die.

Had she waited? Is it possible for people to postpone the time of their deaths? Sociologists have been trying to answer that question for many years. In 1990, a sociologist studied the death rate among elderly Chinese women in California from 1960 to 1984. He discovered that the death rate dropped before the Harvest Moon Festival and then rose: Each year there were fewer deaths than usual the week before the festival and more deaths than usual the week after. The sociologist believed that these changes in the death rate showed the mind's power over the body. The Harvest Moon Festival, when families gather, is important to elderly Chinese women. Apparently, some women were able to postpone their deaths so that they could celebrate the festival one last time. But then, in 2004, another researcher studied the death rate among elderly Chinese women in California during a different time period, from 1985 to 2000. During those years, there were about the same number of deaths before and after the festival. That researcher concluded that Chinese women did not postpone their deaths until after the Harvest Moon Festival.

Sociologists also studied the death rate of elderly Jewish men around the time of Passover. Passover is a Jewish religious holiday that is a family holiday as well. On the first two days of Passover, families gather in their homes for a ceremony. They sit around a table to share a special meal and to listen to the story of Passover. Traditionally, the oldest man in the family sits at the head of the table and reads the story. It is an important event for elderly Jewish men. Sociologists wondered if some Jewish men postponed their deaths until after Passover.

To find out, they studied the death rate among elderly Jewish men in several parts of the world. They discovered that in Connecticut, the death rate dropped before Passover and then rose. That fact seemed to show that Jewish men waited until after Passover to die. But in Israel, the death rate did not change around the holiday, and in California, the death rate actually rose before Passover and then dropped.

The idea that people can postpone the time of their deaths is not new. Many families tell stories of a relative who held on to life until after an important event. They tell of a grandmother who died after the birth of a grandchild, a grandfather who died after his 92nd birthday party. Historians tell stories, too, about famous people like Thomas Jefferson. Jefferson wrote the Declaration of Independence, one of the most important U.S. documents. The Declaration of Independence was signed on July 4, 1776. Jefferson died exactly fifty years later, on July 4, 1826. He died after asking his doctor, "Is it the Fourth?"

continued ▶

All these stories, however, are just that: stories. They are not proof that people can postpone their deaths. The sociologists are studying death rates because death rates are facts, not stories. Only facts can prove that people really can postpone their deaths. So far, the facts haven't proven it.

Still, many nurses and social workers who work with dying people are convinced that people can postpone their deaths, at least for a few days. "We don't know how people stay alive," one social worker says, "and I don't think we'll ever really know, but sometimes they do. We cannot measure the human spirit."

2 VOCABULARY

LOOKING AT THE STORY

Read each sentence. What is the meaning of the word(s) in *italics*? Write the letter of your answer on the line.

_f_ 1. Yinlan was an *elderly* Chinese woman.

_____ 2. She celebrated the Harvest Moon Festival *just* as she had in China.

_____ 3. Her family *gathered* for a special dinner.

_____ 4. She looked at the people sitting around the table and smiled *contentedly*.

_____ 5. When Yinlan died, her family was sad but also *grateful*.

_____ 6. Is it really possible for people to *postpone* their deaths?

_____ 7. Sociologists studied the *death rate* among Chinese women around the time of the festival.

_____ 8. During one time period, the death rate *dropped* before the festival.

_____ 9. Then it *rose* after the festival.

_____ 10. *Apparently* some Chinese women were able to postpone their deaths.

_____ 11. Thomas Jefferson is famous for writing an important U.S. *document*.

_____ 12. Many nurses and social workers are *convinced* that people can postpone their deaths.

a. thankful

b. went up

c. delay

d. happily

e. sure

f. old

g. came together

h. exactly

i. went down

j. it seems

k. paper

l. the number of deaths

LOOKING AT A NEW CONTEXT

A Answer the questions to show that you understand the meanings of the new words. You do not need to write complete sentences.

1. When was the last time your family gathered for a celebration? _____

2. Name someone or something you are grateful for. _____

3. Who is an elderly person that you admire? _____

4. Name something you would like to postpone. _____

5. What is an important document in your country? _____

6. What usually convinces you that something is true? _____

B In a small group, take turns sharing your answers.

3 COMPREHENSION / READING SKILLS
UNDERSTANDING A SUMMARY

The following is a summary of the information in "Does Death Take a Holiday?" Complete the summary. Write your answers on the lines.

Sociologists want to know if people can _____*postpone*_____ the time of their
1.

_____. To find out, they have been studying death
2.

_____ around the time of holidays. For example, they studied the death
3.

rate of _____ women in California around the time of the Harvest
4.

_____ Festival. During the time period from 1960 to 1984, the death rate
5.

_____ before the festival and _____ after it. But during
6.   7.

the years 1985–2000, there were the _____ number of deaths before and
8.

after the festival.

Families tell stories of a _____ who held on to life until after an
9.

_____ event. But the stories are not _____ that people
10.   11.

can postpone their deaths. Sociologists are studying death rates because death rates are

_____, not stories. So far, the death rates have not proven that people can
12.

postpone their deaths.

SCANNING FOR INFORMATION

The underlined information is incorrect. Find the correct information in the story and write it here, above the incorrect information. Work quickly; try to complete this exercise in three minutes or less.

1. Yinlan was ~~88~~ *86* years old.

2. She died ~~five~~ days after the Harvest Moon Festival.

3. Sociologists studied the death rate among elderly Chinese women in ~~Florida~~.

4. They also studied the death rate of elderly Jewish men at the time of ~~Hanukkah~~, a Jewish holiday.

5. On the first ~~three~~ days of Passover, families gather in their homes for a ceremony.

6. In ~~Massachusetts~~, the death rate dropped before Passover and rose after it.

7. But in ~~Russia~~, the death rate did not change, and in California, it actually rose before Passover and dropped after it.

8. Historians tell stories about famous people like ~~William~~ Jefferson.

9. Jefferson was the author of the ~~Bill of Rights~~, one of the most important U.S. documents.

10. The Declaration of Independence was signed on July 4, ~~1774~~.

11. Jefferson died exactly ~~forty~~ years later.

12. Many nurses and social workers who work with dying people are convinced that people can postpone their deaths, at least for a few ~~weeks~~.

4 DISCUSSION

Discuss the following questions with your classmates.

1. One question in the pre-reading exercise was: "Do you think that people can control the time of their own deaths?" After reading the story, is your answer to that question still the same, or has it changed?

2. Do you think the mind has power over the body? Do you think, for example, that people can control whether or not they get sick or feel pain?

3. The Harvest Moon Festival is important to elderly Chinese women because their families gather for a special meal. Passover is important to elderly Jewish men because they sit at the head of the table and tell the story of Passover. Which holiday is important to the elderly people in your family? Why is it important to them?

4. Thomas Jefferson died on July 4, 1826, exactly fifty years after the Declaration of Independence was signed. Do you think it was just a coincidence? Or do you think Jefferson postponed his death until the Fourth of July?

5 WRITING

The sociologists believe that their studies show the mind's power over the body.

A Have you ever used your mind to control your body? Do you know a story that shows that the mind can control the body? Write one or two paragraphs. Here is what one student wrote.

I read a story in the newspaper about an elderly woman who was dying in a hospital. She asked the doctor to call her only son because she wanted to see him one last time. But before her son arrived, the woman's heart stopped beating. The doctor met the woman's son in the lobby of the hospital and told him that his mother had died. When the son went to his mother's room and began to cry, a machine connected to the woman showed that the woman's heart was beating again. The woman opened her eyes, looked at her son, and smiled. A few minutes later, she peacefully left the world again.

B Write about a holiday that is important to you. How do you celebrate it? Here is what one student wrote.

When I was a little girl, my favorite day was March 3. That is when people in Japan celebrate Hinamatsuri, a holiday for girls. The girls dress dolls in beautiful dresses called kimonos and display the dolls. Girls usually get the dolls ready about a week before the holiday. (People say that girls who dress their dolls early get married early, but that wasn't true for me! I always dressed my dolls early, but I am 26 years old and not married.) The first time a girl celebrates Hinamatsuri, her relatives come to her house. Everybody drinks "Shirozake," a special drink, and eats sweets we call "Sakuramochi." The next day, on March 4, the girls put their dolls away. I always felt a little sad when Hinamatsuri was over and it was time to put my dolls away.

CHALLENGE

Guided imagery helps people use the power of the mind to make positive changes in the body. In the two readings in this section, you will learn about guided imagery and experience it for yourself.

A Imagine the situation below.

You have a friend—let's say his name is Sam—who is afraid of taking tests. Sam always studies hard, but often panics when he takes an exam. His mind goes blank, and he can't remember anything. Next week, Sam has a big exam. He's going to study for the exam, of course, but he's also going to prepare for the exam using guided imagery. For fifteen minutes every day, he's going to imagine himself taking the exam. He's going to close his eyes and see himself walking into the classroom. He's going to feel the pencil in his hand and see the exam on his desk. He's going to imagine feeling calm and confident as he writes the answers.

B Do you think this preparation will help Sam? Circle the letter of your answer.

a. Yes, definitely.   b. Probably.   c. Maybe.   d. Probably not.   e. Definitely not.

C Read the article.

Mind over Matter?

Many people believe that the mind has so much power over the body that people can postpone the time of their deaths. So far, sociologists have not been able to prove that this is true. Still, most researchers do not deny that there is a connection between the mind and the body. If you'd like to experience the mind–body connection yourself, do this simple experiment:

Imagine that you are standing in the kitchen. Take a few minutes to look around the kitchen you see in your mind. Notice the color of the kitchen table, appliances, and cupboards. Notice, too, any kitchen sounds, like the hum of the refrigerator. Notice any smells. Now imagine that a cutting board is in front of you. Next to it is a sharp knife.

Next, imagine that on the cutting board there is a plump, fresh, juicy lemon. In your mind, hold the lemon in one hand. Then put it back on the board. Carefully cut it in half with the knife. Now look at the two halves of the lemon. Notice the yellow pulp and the white inner peel. Carefully cut one of the two halves in two. Imagine lifting this lemon wedge to your mouth and smelling it. Now bite into the sour, juicy lemon.

Is your mouth watering? If you're like most people, it is.

You have just experienced guided imagery. Guided imagery uses the power of the mind to cause physical changes in the body. You see, hear, feel, and taste things in your imagination, and your body reacts. (It is called "guided" imagery because usually someone else tells you what to imagine.) Champion athletes have been using guided imagery for years. Before they compete, they repeatedly visualize themselves performing calmly and perfectly. The benefits of guided imagery are so accepted in the world of sports that three out of four Olympic athletes now practice some form of guided imagery.

More recently, doctors have begun using guided imagery with their patients, sometimes with astounding results. Doctors at the Cleveland Clinic in the United States wanted to test the effects of guided imagery on patients who were going to have surgery. So, they did an experiment. They divided 130 patients into two groups. One group (called the "control group") had no special preparation for the surgery. The other group listened to guided imagery tapes for three days before and six days after surgery.

With a background of soothing music, the tapes instructed patients to imagine that they were in calm, beautiful surroundings with someone they loved beside them. Then they were encouraged to imagine themselves in the operating room, having the surgery with little pain or fear.

On the day of the surgery, all patients were asked to rate their anxiety level on a scale from 0 to 100, with 0 meaning no anxiety and 100 meaning extreme anxiety. The control group rated their anxiety as 73; the guided imagery group rated their anxiety as 38. Five days after surgery, the difference between the two groups was even more dramatic. The control group rated their anxiety as 55, whereas the guided imagery group rated their anxiety as 10. The guided imagery group not only felt less anxious, they apparently felt less pain. All patients had medication pumps that allowed them to give themselves painkillers as they needed them. The guided imagery group used 37 percent less pain medicine.

The doctors were especially interested in knowing how much pain medicine their patients used because that amount is an objective, measurable quantity. It is a fact that seems to demonstrate the mind's power over the body.

D Has this article changed your opinion about Sam's use of guided imagery to prepare for the test? Why or why not? Explain your opinion in a small group.

E The guided imagery script below is for people who want to relax. Your teacher is going to read it aloud. Your teacher will pause after each paragraph. If you want to experience how guided imagery works, listen and follow the directions.

A Peaceful Place

Make yourself comfortable. Feel the chair supporting you. Close your eyes.

Relax your eyes. Breathe in…breathe out. Relax your mouth. Smile a little. Breathe in…breathe out. Relax your shoulders. Breathe in…breathe out.

Imagine a place where you feel calm and peaceful. It can be a real place or not real. It can be a place in your past or a place where you've always wanted to go.

Look around the place that you see in your mind. Look left, and then look right. Notice everything you see. Notice every color.

Listen to the sounds of this place. Maybe you hear waves on the beach or wind in the trees. Maybe you hear birds or insects. Maybe you hear children laughing or people singing.

Notice the smells of this place. Maybe you smell flowers, grass, pine trees, rain, or the sea air. Maybe you are in a favorite room, and you smell your favorite food cooking.

Notice how this place feels. Feel the ground beneath your feet. Feel the sand, the dirt, or the grass. Maybe you feel the sun on your face, or maybe you feel a breeze. Feel the temperature of the air. Maybe it is warm, or maybe it is cool. Maybe you are sitting on a warm rock. Feel the rock under your hands. Or maybe you are sitting in a comfortable chair. Feel the soft chair with your hands.

Smile. Breathe in…breathe out. You feel calm, peaceful, and relaxed. You have a feeling that something wonderful is going to happen.

Open your eyes, knowing that you can return to this place at any time.

F Do you feel more relaxed now? If you would like to, share your experience with the class.

G Choose from the following writing activities.

1. Write a guided imagery script for Sam, the young man who panics during tests.

2. Write a guided imagery script for yourself. Imagine a place where you feel calm and peaceful. Describe what you see, hear, smell, and feel.

UNIT 15

1 PRE-READING

Think about these questions. Discuss your answers with your classmates.

1. What is the meaning of the word *sucker*? Read the following definition and example. The dictionary defines *sucker* as "a foolish person who is easily cheated." It is not a polite word. Here is an example of something a sucker might do:

   > A man is selling watches on a busy street in New York City. He is selling them for only twenty dollars each. He says the watches were made by a famous company. When people stop to look, he shows them the company's name on the watch. Someone who believes the man and buys a watch is probably a *sucker*.

2. In your native language, do you have a word similar to the word *sucker*? What is the word? Tell the class.

3. The people in the next story celebrate "Sucker Day." What could this story be about?

Sucker Day

In August 1950, a stranger drove into the small town of Wetumka, Oklahoma. He walked into the local newspaper office and introduced himself. He said that his name was F. Morrison and that he was the publicity man for a circus—a big circus, with elephants, tigers, clowns, and acrobats. He had exciting news: The circus was coming to Wetumka! It would arrive in just three weeks, on August 24.

Wetumka was a town of only 2,000 people, and news traveled fast. By late that afternoon, almost everyone in town had heard about the circus. The businesspeople were especially eager to hear more. A circus would bring people to town, and people would spend money in local stores and restaurants. The businesspeople wanted more information about the circus. Did Mr. Morrison have a few minutes to talk to them?

He sure did! He'd be happy to talk to them! He could meet with them at seven o'clock that evening.

At seven o'clock, the businesspeople of Wetumka gathered to hear about the circus. F. Morrison told them that the circus would attract thousands of people, so they'd better get plenty of supplies. And, he added, he wanted to tell them about a special business opportunity.

"Each person who comes to the circus will get a program," he said, "and in those programs, there will be advertisements. I can sell you advertising space right now." The cautious businesspeople of Wetumka looked at Mr. Morrison and said nothing. "I know, I know. You want to think it over," Mr. Morrison continued. "That's understandable, because advertising space is expensive—in fact, it's very expensive." The businesspeople looked at one another and frowned. "But," he went on, "you'll get more for your money than just advertising space. The circus will buy all its supplies from the businesses that advertise in the program."

"Let me give you an example. A circus sells hot dogs, right? Well, where is the circus going to buy those hot dogs? From the store that advertises in the program! Balloons? Soft drinks? Hay for the elephants? We'll buy them all from the businesses that advertise in the program. And when the circus people get hungry, where will they eat? That's right! At the restaurants that advertise in the program!"

Mr. Morrison told the businesspeople they didn't have to make up their minds right away. He'd be in town for the next two weeks, doing publicity for the circus. They could pay him for advertising space anytime.

During the next two weeks, Mr. Morrison sold advertising space to almost every business in Wetumka. He also became a local hero. He was a friendly man who spent his days walking up and down Main Street, greeting people by name. When it was time for him to leave—he said he had to get back to the circus—people were sorry to see him go. He told everyone he would come back in a week, leading the circus into town. When he left Wetumka, his suitcase was filled with the money that people had paid for advertising space.

On the morning of August 24, crowds of people poured into Wetumka, just as F. Morrison had predicted. By late morning, thousands of people were waiting along Main Street to watch for the circus, which was to arrive at noon.

At noon the circus was nowhere in sight.

At one o'clock, the circus still hadn't come, and the businesspeople realized that they had been tricked. There was no circus! What suckers they were! F. Morrison had cheated them out of their money. But the money was the least of their worries. What were they going to do now about the thousands of people who were waiting for the circus? The crowd was getting more impatient by the minute. What if the hot, tired people became really angry?

The mayor of Wetumka made a quick and wise decision. He told the people that, unfortunately, no circus was coming. Then he immediately declared August 24 "Sucker Day" in Wetumka. He announced that all refreshments were free! The hot dogs, the soft drinks, the ice cream—all free!

continued ▶

This pleased the people so much that they went into local businesses and spent all the money they had brought for the circus. The town businesspeople watched in amazement as their cash registers filled with money.

"Sucker Day" was so successful that the residents of Wetumka decided to celebrate August 24 every year as Sucker Day. There is a parade and free refreshments. It is the biggest event of the year in little Wetumka.

A few years after F. Morrison's visit, the Wetumka police got a phone call from a sheriff in a small town in Missouri. The sheriff said a man named F. Morrison had just been arrested. Mr. Morrison had sold advertising space in a circus program, but there was no circus. Hadn't he pulled the same trick in Wetumka a few years back? Should the sheriff send Morrison to Oklahoma when he finished his jail sentence in Missouri?

The police chief consulted the businesspeople of Wetumka and then phoned the sheriff in Missouri. No, the people of Wetumka didn't want to bring charges against F. Morrison. Mr. Morrison, they said, was the best thing that had ever happened to Wetumka, Oklahoma.

2 VOCABULARY

LOOKING AT THE STORY

Complete the sentences with the words below.

amazement	attract	eager	greeted	sentence
announced	cautious	frowned	impatient	supplies
arrested	consulted	gathered	nowhere in sight	

1. When the businesspeople of Wetumka heard that a circus was coming to town, they were very interested. They were _____ *eager* _____ to hear more.

2. At seven o'clock, the businesspeople came together at the town meeting hall. They _____ to listen to Mr. Morrison.

3. The circus would bring a lot of people to Wetumka. Morrison said it would _____ thousands.

4. Morrison said that businesses should buy all the things they needed for crowds of people. "You should get plenty of _____," he said.

5. The businesspeople didn't smile when Morrison said that advertising space was very expensive. They all _____.

6. The businesspeople were very careful with their money. They were _____ people.

7. As Morrison walked up and down Main Street, he said hello to everyone. He _____ everyone by name.

8. The people were tired of waiting for the circus. They were getting more _____ by the minute.

9. The people looked up and down the street, but they didn't see any elephants, clowns, or acrobats. The circus was _____.

10. After he declared August 24 "Sucker Day," the mayor _____ that all refreshments were free.

11. It was a big surprise to the businesspeople of Wetumka that they made money on August 24. They watched in _____ as their cash registers filled.

12. A sheriff in Missouri took Morrison and put him in jail. After the sheriff _____ Morrison, he called the police chief in Wetumka.

13. Morrison's punishment was one year in jail. The sheriff asked, "Should I send him to Oklahoma when he finishes his _____ here?"

14. The police chief asked the businesspeople of Wetumka for their opinion. After he _____ them, he phoned the sheriff in Missouri.

LOOKING AT SPECIAL EXPRESSIONS

Find the best way to complete or follow each sentence. Write the letter of your answer on the line.

'd better = should

1. Morrison told the businesspeople that the circus would attract thousands of people, so they'd better __c__

2. I'm going on vacation tomorrow, so I'd better _____

3. She has a big test tomorrow, so she'd better _____

a. stay home and study tonight.

b. pack my suitcase.

c. get plenty of supplies.

to make up your mind = to decide

4. Morrison told the businesspeople that they could buy advertising space anytime; _____

5. The little boy stood at the ice cream stand for five minutes; _____

6. She can't decide whether to stay in her apartment or look for a better place; _____

d. finally, his mother told him he had to make up his mind and choose a flavor.

e. the landlord is giving her until June to make up her mind.

f. they didn't have to make up their minds right away.

the least of your worries = a problem that is less important than another one

7. The money was the least of their worries. _____

8. The burned cake was the least of their worries. _____

9. The stolen jacket was the least of his worries. _____

g. The expensive baking pan they'd borrowed was ruined.

h. Who had the student ID that was in the pocket?

i. What were they going to do now about the thousands of people who were waiting for the circus?

3 COMPREHENSION/READING SKILLS

UNDERSTANDING THE MAIN IDEAS

Circle the letter of the best answer.

1. Who was F. Morrison?
   a. He was the publicity man for a circus.
   b. He was the editor of the newspaper in Wetumka, Oklahoma.
   c. He was a man who cheated people out of their money.

2. Why were the businesspeople eager to hear about the circus?
   a. A circus would bring people to Wetumka, and these people would spend money in local stores and restaurants.
   b. Most of the businesspeople had children who would enjoy the circus.
   c. Wetumka was very small, so there wasn't much to do; a circus would bring some excitement to the town.

3. Why were the businesspeople willing to pay a lot of money for advertising space in the circus program?
   a. Buying advertising space in the circus program was cheaper than other types of advertising.
   b. They thought that a lot of people would see their advertisements.
   c. Morrison told them that the circus would buy its supplies from the businesses that advertised in the program.

4. How successful was F. Morrison at selling advertising space?
   a. Almost every business in Wetumka bought advertising space.
   b. About half the businesses in Wetumka bought advertising space.
   c. The cautious businesspeople in Wetumka didn't buy advertising space, but Morrison was very successful in Missouri.

5. When the circus didn't come, what was the biggest worry of the businesspeople?
   a. They worried most about the money they had lost.
   b. They worried most about selling all the supplies they had bought.
   c. They worried most about the crowd of hot, impatient people.

6. What did the mayor of Wetumka tell the angry crowd?
   a. He promised them that the circus would be there soon.
   b. He announced that all the refreshments were free.
   c. He told them that Morrison had been arrested in Missouri.

7. How do the people of Wetumka celebrate Sucker Day every year?
   a. There is a parade and free refreshments.
   b. There is a free circus.
   c. There is music and dancing.

SCANNING FOR INFORMATION

The underlined information is incorrect. Find the correct information in the story and write it here, above the incorrect information. Work quickly; try to complete this exercise in three minutes or less.

1. In August ~~1952~~ *1950*, a stranger drove into the small town of Wetumka, Oklahoma.

2. He walked into the local <u>real estate</u> office and introduced himself.

3. He said that his name was <u>M.</u> Morrison.

4. Morrison said that a circus would arrive on August <u>23</u>.

5. Morrison said he'd be in town for <u>three</u> weeks, doing publicity for the circus.

6. When Morrison left Wetumka, his <u>briefcase</u> was filled with the money people had paid for advertising space.

7. Thousands of people were waiting along Main Street to watch for the circus, which was to arrive at <u>one o'clock</u>.

8. The <u>police chief</u> of Wetumka declared August 24 Sucker Day.

9. Several years after F. Morrison's visit, the Wetumka police got a call from a sheriff in <u>Kansas</u>.

10. The police chief consulted the businesspeople of Wetumka and then <u>wrote</u> the sheriff that they didn't want to bring charges against Morrison.

RETELLING A STORY

Imagine this: You live in Wetumka, Oklahoma. You are watching the annual Sucker Day parade. Two visitors to Wetumka are standing next to you. They ask, "Why do you call this celebration Sucker Day?" How do you answer? Complete the explanation below on your own paper.

In 1950, a man named F. Morrison came to Wetumka. He said he was the publicity man for a circus that would arrive on August 24. . . .

4 DISCUSSION

A Look at the poster below for Sucker Day in Wetumka. Then make a poster for a festival that you have attended. Draw a picture on your poster and be sure to include:

- the name of the festival
- the place
- the date (You can make up a date.)
- the events and the time of each event

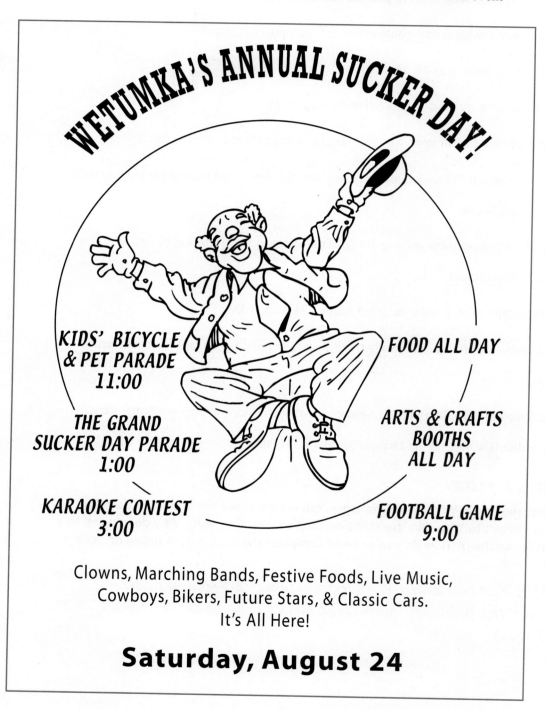

WETUMKA'S ANNUAL SUCKER DAY!

KIDS' BICYCLE
& PET PARADE
11:00

THE GRAND
SUCKER DAY PARADE
1:00

KARAOKE CONTEST
3:00

FOOD ALL DAY

ARTS & CRAFTS
BOOTHS
ALL DAY

FOOTBALL GAME
9:00

Clowns, Marching Bands, Festive Foods, Live Music,
Cowboys, Bikers, Future Stars, & Classic Cars.
It's All Here!

Saturday, August 24

B Display your poster in the classroom. Answer your classmates' questions about the festival.

C   Interview a classmate who has information about an unusual festival. Ask your classmate the questions below. Listen carefully and take notes when your classmate answers.

1. What is the name of the festival?
2. Where is it?
3. When is it?
4. How many people go to the festival?
5. What happens at the festival?
6. Do people wear special clothes?
7. Do people eat special foods?
8. Do people play games?
9. Is there music?
10. Do you know the history of the festival?
11. Have you ever gone to the festival?

5 WRITING

A   Using the information your classmate gave you in Exercise 4C, write a paragraph about an unusual festival. Or write about an unusual festival that you have attended. Here is what one student wrote.

The first weekend in July, our little village in Lichtenhorst, Germany, follows a very old tradition and celebrates its annual "Schützenfest." It is in honor of the people in our village who are the best at shooting a rifle.

The most important person of the Schützenfest is the champion shooter (Schützenkönig). He is crowned a few days before the Schützenfest. All male members of the shooting club shoot at a target and try to get a score of 10 three times. The man who gets a score of 30 is crowned Schützenkönig.

Late on Friday afternoon, almost everyone in our village meets at the village hall to march together to the champion shooter's home. He receives a medal and delivers a little speech before inviting all his guests to have drinks, ice cream, and candy with him and his family.

Afterward everyone marches back to the village hall and the fun part begins. Everyone celebrates by having a big dinner together. A band plays and the waiters are busy carrying huge plates of food to each table. As soon as the dinner is over, people start to dance, and the party goes on until late into the night.

When the music stops, people go home looking forward to next year's Schützenfest in Lichtenhorst.

B   Write the true story of someone you know who was cheated out of his or her money. Or write about an experience you thought was going to be bad but turned out well in the end.

F. Morrison told the businesspeople of Wetumka that he had a special opportunity for them. His "business opportunity" was a scam (a dishonest trick), and the businesspeople of Wetumka lost a lot of their money.

A Read about other opportunities that could also be scams.

1 Get Paid to Shop

We are a company in the mystery shopper field, and we are hiring mystery shoppers.

Job Description: You will be assigned to visit stores and businesses. You will pretend to be a potential customer who is looking for a specific product or service. You will then complete an online questionnaire to share with us your experience as a customer. You will be paid $350 for each assignment. We guarantee at least two assignments per week.

Requirements: (1) age 18 or above; (2) can speak the local language well; (3) can read and write English.

How to Apply: Fill out the attached registration form. Your address will help us match you with the location of stores and businesses in your area. We will also use this address to send payments to you.

Training: This position requires a one-hour online training session. The fee for the session is $100. Once we receive your registration form and the $100 fee, we will send you a link to the online training session. After you complete the training, you'll receive your first assignment.

Then you can start getting paid to shop!

2 Models Needed

Earn $100 per hour or $500 per day as a fashion or commercial model. Full- or part-time. No experience necessary. Real-people types, such as children, grandmothers, college students, and construction workers welcome. No fee.

Call now to schedule an interview. If you are selected, we will ask you to provide professional photographs. We will distribute your photos to businesses that are looking for "real-people" models—people like YOU!

3 $2,000 Scholarship Guaranteed

Every year, millions of dollars in scholarships go unclaimed. You can use this money to finance your college education. Simply pay us a $200 scholarship fee, and we will scan our electronic database and match you with a scholarship. If we can't find at least a $2,000 scholarship for you, we will return your $200.

4 Final Notification
* * * * *
Brand-New Car

This is our final notification regarding a brand-new car we will deliver directly to you. The car is being held in a secured facility awaiting your response. Failure to respond by the posted deadline date will result in forfeiture of the car. First, choose the car you would like:

☐ Ford Mustang   ☐ Honda Accord

☐ Hyundai Elantra   ☐ Toyota Camry

☐ Chevrolet Cruze   ☐ Dodge Charger

Then send $21.99 to cover the cost of delivery of your car. This is a nationwide offer to promote the sale of new 1:39-scale model cars. Send $21.99 today to guarantee delivery of the car of your choice.

5 Surprise Gifts in Your Mailbox!

Couldn't we all use a surprise gift? My friend did this last year, and I couldn't believe how well it worked!

Here's how to get a surprise gift in your mailbox. I don't care where you live—you're welcome to join in the secret gift exchange. You only have to buy one gift valued at $10 or more and send it to one secret friend. (I'll send you the address.) Then add your name to the list, and you will receive up to 36 gifts in return. Let me know if you are interested, and I will send you the information by private message. Don't ask to participate if you're not willing to send a gift because it messes up the cycle for the others. Just comment to this post if you're in, and I will send you a private message with instructions.

B   Circle the numbers of the opportunities that you think are scams. Then check the Key on page 138 to find out which are scams.

Mirsada Buric

1 PRE-READING

The woman in the picture is running through the streets of her city, Sarajevo, in 1992.

Look at the picture and think about these questions. Discuss your answers with your classmates.

1. In what country is Sarajevo?

2. Why do you think the woman is running?

3. Look at the building behind the woman. What do you think happened to the building? Take a guess. (Remember that any logical guess is correct.)

Love under Siege

On a Sunday afternoon in the summer of 1992, Eric Adam sat folding laundry in his apartment in Phoenix, Arizona. He was half listening to the news on TV and trying not to think back.

Two years ago, Eric had been happy; he was engaged to marry a wonderful woman named Suzi. But Eric's happiness ended suddenly. Suzi, who had a weak heart, died of a heart attack. She was 33 years old. Now, two years after Suzi's death, Eric was still struggling with his grief. As he sat on his sofa, folding laundry, his thoughts kept returning to Suzi.

The news on TV was about the summer Olympics. A reporter was talking about a young woman from Bosnia. She was a runner who was training for the Olympics. Twice a day, she ran through the streets of Sarajevo. "Sarajevo?" Eric wondered. There was a civil war going on in the city of Sarajevo. How could anyone train for the Olympics in Sarajevo? Eric stopped folding laundry and looked at the TV. On the screen, a young woman was running through Sarajevo's streets. She was running with her head held high, even though snipers occasionally tried to shoot her. She ran straight toward the camera and then she was gone. The news report was over.

Eric stared at the TV screen. He was stunned. What courage the woman had! Eric wanted to meet this woman; he wanted to talk to her. That wouldn't be easy. She lived halfway around the world, and Eric didn't even know her name.

Eric went to the library and began looking through newspapers. Finally, he found what he was looking for—a photo of the young woman running through the streets of Sarajevo. Under the photo was the woman's name: Mirsada Buric. From the newspapers, Eric learned that Mirsada was no longer in Sarajevo. She was at the Summer Olympic Games in Barcelona, Spain.

Eric wrote Mirsada a letter. He wrote that he had seen her on TV and wanted her to know that "there is someone in America who admires you." He ended his letter, "If I can help you in any way, please let me know."

Mirsada's Olympic race was the 3,000 meters. Mirsada didn't win, but when she crossed the finish line, the people in the stadium stood and cheered. They had seen Mirsada on TV, running through the streets of Sarajevo. In the eyes of the crowd, Mirsada was a winner.

After the Olympics, Mirsada couldn't return to Sarajevo because it was too dangerous. She went to Slovenia, a country north of Bosnia, as a refugee. Separated from her family, Mirsada was lonely. She thought about Eric's letter and decided to answer it, with the help of her Bosnian-English dictionary. Eric answered her letter and sent a picture of himself. For the next few months, letters flew back and forth between Eric and Mirsada. Finally, Eric wrote Mirsada that he was going to be in Europe on business. He wanted to stop in Slovenia so that he could meet her.

At nine o'clock in the evening, Mirsada stood on a street corner in Slovenia, waiting for Eric. A small car pulled up, and a young man with brown hair and blue eyes stepped out of the car. It was Eric. He ran to Mirsada, smiling. "How are you?" Eric asked. "Fine," Mirsada answered. Then they looked at each other and laughed. Eric couldn't speak Bosnian, and Mirsada couldn't speak English. Eric went to the car and got the woman who was interpreting for him.

Mirsada, Eric, and the interpreter went to Mirsada's small apartment, where Eric and Mirsada began to talk. They talked until sunrise. Then Eric had to go. If he didn't leave within the hour, he would miss his flight back to the United States. As he walked toward the car, Eric saw the sadness in Mirsada's eyes. Suddenly he said, "Do you want to come to the United States? There'd be no strings attached—I'll buy a round-trip ticket, so you can go home anytime." Mirsada began to cry. "No," she answered. "Thank you. But no." Eric kissed Mirsada on the cheek and said, "Well, if you ever change your mind, the offer stands." Then he was gone.

Mirsada thought about Eric's offer for weeks. Finally, she decided to go to the United States.

In March 1993, nine months after Eric first saw her on TV, Mirsada arrived in Phoenix,

continued ▶

Arizona. She moved into Eric's apartment, where she and Eric lived together like a brother and a sister. Mirsada studied English. She started college classes. She ran in dozens of races and won most of them. And, she fell in love with Eric, who was already in love with her. In December, they were married.

In the summer of 1996, the Olympic torch passed through Phoenix, Arizona, on its way to the Games in Atlanta, Georgia. Mirsada was chosen to carry the torch through Phoenix. As Mirsada ran through the cheering crowd, she thought about everything she had done since the last Olympics. She had come to the United States, learned English, and graduated from college. She had won races. She had fallen in love and gotten married. And now she was carrying the Olympic torch through the streets of Phoenix. She ran as she had run through the streets of Sarajevo—with her head held high.

2 VOCABULARY

LOOKING AT THE STORY

Complete the sentences with the words below.

admires	engaged	no strings attached	stunned
cheered	grief	occasionally	thoughts kept returning
courage	laundry	refugee	trained

1. Eric washed his clothes. Then he sat on the sofa and folded his _____laundry_____.

2. Eric was going to get married. He was _____ to a woman named Suzi.

3. Eric was fighting his feelings of sadness about Suzi's death. He was still struggling with his _____.

4. Eric couldn't stop thinking about Suzi. His _____ to her.

5. The runner on TV was preparing for the Olympics. She _____ by running through the streets of Sarajevo twice a day.

6. Sometimes, men with guns tried to kill people in Sarajevo. Mirsada ran even though snipers _____ tried to shoot her.

7. Mirsada didn't seem to be afraid. What _____ she had!

8. Eric was very surprised to see a woman running through the streets of Sarajevo; he couldn't believe it. When the news report was over, he stared at the TV screen and didn't move. He was _____.

9. After seeing her on TV, Eric had a high opinion of Mirsada. He wrote her, "Someone in the United States _____ you."

10. When Mirsada crossed the finish line, the people in the stadium shouted with happiness. They _____ because they knew Mirsada; they had seen her on TV, running through the streets of Sarajevo.

11. Mirsada couldn't return to her country because it was too dangerous. So, she went to Slovenia as a _____.

12. Eric told Mirsada he would buy her a round-trip ticket to the United States. He didn't want anything from her in return. He told her that there would be _____.

LOOKING AT A NEW CONTEXT

A Complete the sentences to show that you understand the meanings of the new words.

1. Something I do only occasionally is _____.

2. Someone whose courage I admire is _____.

3. A sports team I cheer for is _____.

4. An Olympic sport I would love to train for is _____.

5. A person my thoughts keep returning to is _____.

6. A place my thoughts keep returning to is _____.

7. I would be stunned if _____.

8. There are a lot of news reports about refugees from _____.

9. The right amount of time for couples to be engaged before they get married is _____

_____.

B In a small group, take turns reading your sentences aloud. When your classmates read their answers, follow up with comments and questions, such as "Really?" "Why?" or "Me too."

3 COMPREHENSION/READING SKILLS

UNDERSTANDING CAUSE AND EFFECT

Find the best way to complete each sentence. Write the letter of your answer on the line.

1. Eric was struggling with grief _d_

2. Eric couldn't believe a runner was training in Sarajevo _____

3. Eric wanted to meet Mirsada _____

4. For a week, Eric looked through newspapers _____

5. As she ran through the streets of Phoenix, Mirsada held her head high _____

a. because he wanted to know the name of the Bosnian runner he had seen on TV.

b. because there was a war there.

c. because she was proud of everything she had done.

d. because Suzi had died.

e. because he admired her courage.

UNDERSTANDING SUPPORTING DETAILS

Read each sentence on the left. Which sentence on the right gives you more information? Match the sentences. Write the letter of your answer on the line.

_b_ 1. Eric was happy.

_____ 2. The reporter on TV was talking about a young woman from Bosnia.

_____ 3. Eric sent Mirsada a letter.

_____ 4. Mirsada's race was the 3,000 meters.

_____ 5. Mirsada thought about everything she had done.

a. She was a runner who was training for the Olympics by running through the streets of Sarajevo twice a day.

b. He was engaged to marry a wonderful woman named Suzi.

c. He wrote that he had seen Mirsada on TV and that he admired her.

d. She had come to the United States, learned English, graduated from college, won races, fallen in love, and gotten married.

e. She didn't win, but people cheered when she crossed the finish line.

4 DISCUSSION

Eric introduced himself to Mirsada in a letter after seeing her on TV. Later he flew to Slovenia, and they met in person. That is an unusual way for a couple to meet!

A **With the help of your classmates and your teacher, make a list of questions you could ask someone who is married about how he or she met his or her wife or husband.**

• How old were you when you met?

• Where did you meet?

• What did you think when you saw her or him for the first time?

• _____

• _____

• _____

B **Ask someone who is married the questions. Listen carefully and write down the answers. Then tell the class what you learned.**

C **What about you and your spouse (if you are married)? Your parents? Your grandparents? In a small group, tell the story of how you or they met.**

5 WRITING

The story of Mirsada Buric is a story about love. It is also about the many challenges she had in her life.

Choose one of the following writing activities.

1. Write the love story of how you met your spouse, or how someone you know met his or her spouse. Here is what one student wrote.

When I was 24 years old, I came to the United States from Mexico to live with my aunt. I was her housekeeper. My aunt and her sons treated me very badly. My day started at 5:00 a.m. I had to cook all their meals, clean their shoes, and pick up their clothes. I had to clean the house very well because when my aunt came home, she wiped her hand over the furniture looking for dust. When everybody went to sleep, I began to iron.

In the spring, I did the ironing on an enclosed porch with lots of windows. Every night, a young man stood on the porch next door and watched me iron, but he never spoke to me.

One summer day, I went to the store, and he started walking by my side. For the first time, he spoke to me. He wondered why they treated me so badly. His house was so close that he could hear when they screamed at me. He told me if I wanted to go back to Mexico, he would buy me an airplane ticket, but I did not go. I needed the $10 a week that my aunt paid me and that I sent to my family in Mexico.

That was 29 years ago. I am married to the man who was looking at me on the porch. We celebrated our 28th anniversary. I love him very much. He is a caring man with a big heart, and he is a wonderful father and husband. I thank God for him.

2. Write about a challenge you had in your life. Here is what one student wrote.

When my son was 12 years old, he was in an accident. A car hit him. When I arrived at the hospital, he was unconscious. The doctor told me, "He will probably never walk or talk again. He will probably never go to school or have a job."

I quit my job and stayed home to take care of my son. I took him swimming a lot. In one year, he recovered completely from the accident.

My son is 31 years old now. He is a journalist.

Mirsada Buric did not win the 3,000-meter race at the Olympics—she finished thirty-first out of thirty-three runners—yet her race is considered one of the great moments in Olympic history.

A **Read the beginning of three stories about great Olympic moments.**

1 Kip Keino, Kenya, Track and Field

On the morning of his 1,500-meter race at the 1968 Games, runner Kip Keino of Kenya was riding in a taxi to the Olympic Stadium in Mexico City. He was worried. There were traffic jams all over the city, and his taxi was barely moving. Keino kept looking ahead at the cars, buses, and taxis in front of him, and then down at his watch. It was an hour before his race, then fifty minutes, then forty minutes, then thirty minutes. Finally, it was only twenty minutes before the start of the race. And the taxi was still 2 kilometers from the stadium.

For the past several days, Keino had been suffering from severe stomach pains, and doctors thought he probably had an infection. Earlier that morning, he had been worried that he might not run well. Now he was worried that he might

not run at all. At the rate the taxi was traveling, he couldn't possibly get to the race on time.

2 Vera Caslavska, Czechoslovakia (now the Czech Republic), Gymnastics

Gymnast Vera Caslavska had won three gold medals and one silver medal at the 1964 Games in Tokyo, and she was the favorite to win again at the Games in Mexico City in 1968. But just a few months before the Games, politics almost prevented her from competing in the Olympics at all.

In 1968, Czechoslovakia (now the Czech Republic) was still controlled by the Soviet Union. Many people in Czechoslovakia, including Caslavska, wanted to be free of that control. In April 1968, she signed a document called the "Manifesto of 2,000 Words," which demanded Czechoslovakia's independence from the Soviet Union. A short time later, Soviet tanks rolled into Prague. Caslavska's friends warned her that she was in danger of being arrested, so she went to a small village in the mountains. It was just two months before the Olympics, and

Caslavska needed to practice. But there was no gym in the village and none of the equipment a gymnast needed.

Derek Redmond, Great Britain, Track and Field

Derek Redmond was a great runner who had a lot of injuries. By the time of the 1992 Olympics in Barcelona, he had already had five operations. The latest operation, on his foot, was just four months before the Games began. But he recovered well from the surgery, and in Barcelona, everything seemed to be going his way. He had an excellent chance of winning the gold medal in the 400-meter race.

Redmond easily won the quarterfinal race. Next came the semifinal. Redmond was in the lead as the runners went around the first bend in the track. Suddenly, he felt a sharp pain in the back of his leg and dropped to the ground in agony. A muscle had torn. When he looked up and saw paramedics coming toward him with a stretcher, he made up his mind: They would not carry him off the track. He immediately jumped up and began limping toward the finish line.

B Write the ending of each story. If you don't know the ending, take a guess and write a possible ending.

1. Did Keino get to the race on time? If so, how did he do it?

2. How did Caslavska train for the Olympics? Did she go to the Games in Mexico City? If so, what happened there?

3. Did Redmond finish the semifinal race? If so, how did he do it?

C Check the Key on page 138 to find out the true ending of each story.

KEY TO GUESSED ANSWERS

UNIT 1
DISCUSSION pages 8–9

All of the statements are true.

CHALLENGE pages 10–11

1. Elizabeth Barrett Browning and Robert Browning
2. June Carter Cash and Johnny Cash
3. Anna and Boris Kozlov

UNIT 3
CHALLENGE pages 28–29

1. c	4. c	7. c	10. c
2. b	5. c	8. a	
3. b	6. c	9. a	

UNIT 4
PRE-READING page 30

All of the statements are false.

UNIT 8
CHALLENGE pages 70–71

The items sold for these amounts:

Andy Warhol painting	$11.7 million
Lincoln letter	$442,500
Diana's gown	$200,000
Steiff teddy bear	$38,000

UNIT 10
DISCUSSION page 84

Driving is the most dangerous way to travel.

CHALLENGE pages 86–87

1. c (467/1 – heart disease)
2. e (1,656/1 – all accidents and injuries)
3. b (157,300/1 – falling downstairs)
4. d (2.3 million/1 – storm)
5. a (7 million/1 – plane crash)

UNIT 11
CHALLENGE pages 94–95

The story about the dog that swallowed the cell phone (#4) is true.

UNIT 13
PRE-READING page 104

The photo was taken in the United States, in the state of Pennsylvania, in 2017.

UNIT 15
CHALLENGE pages 128–129

All five "opportunities" are scams.

UNIT 16
CHALLENGE pages 136–137

1. Keino got out of the taxi and ran the 2 kilometers to the stadium. So, while his competitors were resting and preparing themselves mentally for the race, he was jogging through the crowded streets of Mexico City. He arrived at the stadium minutes before the race. He won the 1,500, setting a world record. After the Olympics, he had surgery for an infected gall bladder.

2. Vera continued to practice while living in the village. She kept in shape by swinging from tree branches and practiced her floor exercises in a meadow. In the end, the government allowed her to compete in Mexico City, where she won two gold medals and two silvers. She was a favorite of the crowd, especially after she married fellow Olympian Josef Odiozil in Mexico City.

3. Redmond's father, Jim, was watching the race from the stands. He ran down to the track and, paying no attention to the security guards who tried to stop him, rushed to his son. Derek put his arm around his father. Holding his father's hand and sobbing, Redmond limped toward the finish line. A few feet from the finish line, Redmond let go of his father and finished the race on his own. The crowd of 65,000 gave him a standing ovation.